SIDE HUSTLE 101

100+ IDEAS ON HOW TO REALISTICALLY MAKE
SIX FIGURES WITH PART-TIME GIGS

STEVEN MOSTYN, MBA

First Edition: 2023
Side Hustle 101: 100+ Ideas on How to Realistically Make Six Figures with Part-Time Gigs
This book is dedicated to my cousin Robert Verchick, a great friend who has always been ahead of the curve in life!

About the Author

Steven Mostyn, MBA, is a 5-time bestselling author. He has written eleven books and over 100 articles for leading sites such as Forbes, HR.com, Fast Money, Paradise Media, Recruitment.com, and other forms of media.

For over 25 Years, Steven Mostyn has built a global reputation as a serial entrepreneur, career coach, and owner of multiple consulting companies, including Alpha Recruitment, LP Writers, ML Consulting, Super Star Resume, Career Agents, and Career Boost Group.

Steve earned a bachelor's degree from York University and an MBA with a focus in HR from Centenary University.

Follow Steve on social media or his sites online.

https://www.linkedin.com/in/stevenmostyn

https://www.facebook.com/careerboostgroup

https://twitter.com/top_headhunter

Table of Content

Preface

With inflation causing the cost of living to increase for everyone globally, many people are living paycheck to paycheck. Due to this high inflation, many people are also not able to support themselves or their families. This is why many people need to have part-time streams of income to supplement their incomes just to survive. To me, just surviving is not good enough, and you owe it to yourself and your family to thrive. This is why I wrote this comprehensive step-by-step guide on side hustles in order to provide the general public with a way to learn how to realistically obtain multiple levels of income part-time and even turn these into a full-time career.

About me

I am not just another writer on this topic, as I am a leading global expert on the topic of careers, having written multiple previous related bestsellers on the topic and owning a few career consulting businesses Career Agents, Elite Pro Resume, and Super Star Resume. In addition, many of the ideas outlined in the book I have successfully applied and have made money with.

This book will be no-nonsense and right to the point. Side Hustle 101 was written for the busy person in mind. The writing is clear, the format is simple, and the chapters are brief and straightforward. To get the most out of this book, read it more than once. Apply what you learn and you will have all the skills you need to build your income streams.

Chapter 1:

How to Best Use this Book and Recommendations

Before starting your journey of finding options for your side hustle, I want to explain to you how to use this book.

What information will be provided on each side hustle?

Not all side hustles have the same level of difficulty to perform or have the same starting costs, so for each side hustle listed in this book, I will provide a 5-star rating in terms of their difficulty or the cost associated with the side hustle. For example, if a side hustle is a 5 for both difficulty and 5 for the cost, it means that the side hustle is both difficult to perform and very expensive to start doing. On the flip side, if a side hustle gets a 1 for difficulty and a 1 for cost, it is easy to learn and does not cost anything.

In addition, I will provide the realistic excepted income you can make with each side hustle.

Also listed will be any positives or negatives of each side hustle.

Nothing is Easy!

One very important point I would like to point out is that there is no such thing as an easy get-rich-quick scheme, and all the things I list in this book take work. That being said, many of the side hustle ideas I list in this book are realistic for many people, and it's all about choosing things you are capable of doing and prefer to do.

Do not give up your day job at first!

If you have a day job, my big piece of advice to you is to keep your main source of income before giving that up. Later on, if you like, once you feel comfortable with your sources of income with your side hustle, then you can quit your day job.

Develop multiple streams of income!

One of the things I am known for preaching when it comes to careers or money is always to have multiple streams of income. The reason for this is that you never know when one source of income drops or even your main source of income. In these bad times, you absolutely must create multiple wealth streams to be successful. My favorite saying is to **"be monogamous in your relationship and be polygamous with your income."**

Pick side hustles you can realistically do!

There is a large number of side hustles listed in this book, and my advice is to read them over carefully and choose side hustles you can realistically do based on skills you can already do or can learn as well as costs.

Have a passion or go home!

Having done many side hustles in my life, I will say that if you are not passionate about the space you are going to be doing side hustle in, you most likely will not be successful, let alone make over six figures within that discipline. If you are going to put all the time and effort into building a successful side hustle, you must ensure you choose side hustles that interest you.

Experiment

It might take trying a few of the side hustles listed in this book in order to discover side hustles that interest you, make you money and do not ruin your personal life.

Success is not overnight!

Again, you have to realize that success is not instantaneous, but if you work hard and apply things you learn in this book, you can develop over time excellent ways to make extra income.

Also, please note that I do not endorse or get paid for any of the sites listed in this book.

Chapter 2:

Renting Things You Own Out to Others for Profit

Many people, when they think of renting something they own out, may just think of the popular Airbnb platform of renting out your house for people looking for short-term vacation rental. There are actually many things you can rent out for a profit, and below I will list many you can learn about.

1. Renting a room in your house to a renter

This is something people have been doing for eternity, and the reason is that many people with space they do not need can rent it out for profit.

Where to find tenants: Word of mouth, sign on your property, use a 3rd party agent, post on college sites, post on social media.

How to choose tenants: Get references, do a credit check if possible, a criminal check if possible, and check social media and Google to find anything negative about the person.

Positives: Making money out of a room you do not need.

Negatives: Invasion of privacy, tenants that do not pay, messy person, loud person, renting to a bad person.

Cost: 2/5 - Cost of extra utility usage like water, gas, and electricity, cleaning costs. Possible advertising costs.

Difficulty Level: 1/5 – As long as you choose a good tenant.

Profit Potential: $300 US to over $1,000 a month, depending on region and size of the room.

2. Rent out your place or room for short-term rentals

As mentioned at the beginning of this chapter, Airbnb might be the first thing people think about when renting out something you own. Airbnb and their competitors allow homeowners to rent out their home or a room for people looking for a place to stay short term and usually on vacation.

Positives: Quick money using a room or a house you do not need.

Negatives: Overcrowded market, getting bad tenants, privacy issues.

Cost: 2/5 – Cost of extra utility usage like water, gas, and electricity, cleaning costs.

Difficulty Level: 1/5 – As long as you choose a good tenant.

Profit Potential: $100 a day to over $1,000 – depending on how large your house is and your area.

Tips: To build up reviews, start low, then charge more, and make sure your place is always clean. Use amazing pictures and descriptions.

Different short-term rental sites:

Airbnb – https://www.airbnb.com/

Vrbo – https://www.vrbo.com/

Wimdu – https://www.wimdu.com/

Booking.com - https://www.booking.com/holiday-homes/index.html

Hometogo.com - https://www.hometogo.com/

3. Storage space

Many of us have storage space we do not need. Would you believe there are people who actually pay to have storage space? A site called Neighbor - https://www.neighbor.com/ allows people to make money by renting out their storage space. Another great site is called Store at My House – https://storeatmyhouse.com/

Positives: Quick money using storage space you do not need.

Negatives: Overcrowded market in some areas, getting a bad renter, privacy issues.

Cost: 1/5 – None, as you already have the space.

Difficulty Level: 1/5 – As long as you choose a good renter.

Profit Potential: Garage: Earn between $100-$600 per month.

Closets and rooms in your house - $100 to over $500 a month Driveway: Earn between $50-$150 per month.

Shed: Earn $50-$200 per month.

4. Renting out your swimming pool

If you own a swimming pool, you can rent it out to people who want to use a pool. A site called Swimply - https://swimply.com/become-a-host allows you to rent out your swimming pool.

Positives: Quick money renting out something you may not be fully using.

Negatives: Getting a bad renter, privacy issues.

Cost: 2/5 – Extra cost for pool cleaning and utilities.

Difficulty Level: 1/5 – As long as you have good renters.

Profit Potential: $30 to over $5,000 a month.

5. Renting out garden space

Yes, there are people who will pay you to rent out all or part of your garden to them. A site called Yardyum - https://yardyum.com/ allows people to rent out their gardens to others.

Positives: Quick money renting out something you may not be fully using.

Negatives: Getting a bad renter, privacy issues.

Cost: 1/5 – Most likely a 1 but could be extra water costs.

Difficulty Level: 1/5 – As long as you have good renters.

Profit Potential: $30 to over $100 a month.

6. Renting out your land to campers

Some people looking to camp out are looking to rent land for their campers or tents. A site called Homecamper - https://www.homecamper.com/land/new allows you to rent out your land to campers.

Positives: Quick money renting out something you may not be fully using.

Negatives: Getting a bad renter, privacy issues.

Cost: 2/5 – Most likely a 1 but could be extra utility or cleaning costs.

Difficulty Level: 1/5 – As long as you have good renters.

Profit Potential: $10 to over $1,000 a month.

7. Renting out your driveway space

Some people, especially in overcrowded places, need a parking space and will pay you to rent out theirs. A site called Parqex – https://parqex.com/individuals/ will allow you to rent out your parking space. You can also advertise yourself on social media or put up a sign.

Positives: Quick money renting out something you may not be fully using.

Negatives: Getting a bad renter, privacy issues.

Cost: 1/5 – Should be no added cost to you.

Difficulty Level: 1/5 – As long as you have good renters.

Profit Potential: $285 to $325 a month.

8. Rent your house out for a movie shoot or event

A site called Giggster – https://giggster.com/ allows you to rent out your home for a movie shoot or event.

Positives: Quick money renting out something you may not be fully using.

Negatives: Getting a bad renter, privacy issues.

Cost: 2/5 – Cost of extra utility usage like water, gas, and electricity, cleaning costs.

Difficulty Level: 1/5 – As long as you have good renters.

Profit Potential: $1,000 to over $5,000 for three days.

9. Renting out your yard for other people's pets.

In some areas, there is not enough place for pets to play, so some people will rent yards for their pets. A site called Sniffspot – https://www.sniffspot.com/ allows you to rent your yard to pet owners.

Positives: Quick money renting out something you may not be fully using.

Negatives: Getting a bad renter, privacy issues, messes after pets make.

Cost: 2/5 – Extra utility or cleaning costs.

Difficulty Level: 1/5 – As long as you have good renters.

Profit Potential: $10 to over $1,000 a month.

10. Renting out your car

Not using your car all the time, you can rent out your car for cash with sites like Getaround https://www.getaround.com/.

Positives: Quick money renting out something you may not be fully using.

Negatives: Expensive upkeep, bad renters.

Cost: 3/5 – For the site – $100 for initial setup and $20 per month. Plus, the monthly cost of insurance, maintenance, and depreciation that could be over $500 a month.

Difficulty Level: 1/5 – As long as you have good renters.

Profit Potential: $100 to over $1,000 a month.

11. Renting out your motorcycle

Just like your car, you can also rent out your motorcycle with sites like Riders-share <u>https://www.riders-share.com/</u>

Positives: Quick money renting out something you may not be fully using.

Negatives: Expensive upkeep, bad renters.

Cost: 3/5 – Monthly cost of insurance, maintenance, and depreciation could be over $200 a month.

Difficulty Level: 1/5 – As long as you have good renters.

Profit Potential: $80 to over $200 per month per motorcycle.

12. Renting out your truck

Many people need trucks for various reasons, and sites like fetchtruck allow you to rent out your trucks. https://fetchtruck.com/

Positives: Quick money renting out something you may not be fully using.

Negatives: Expensive upkeep, bad renters.

Cost: 3/5 – Monthly cost of insurance, maintenance, and depreciation could be over $700 a month.

Difficulty Level: 1/5 – As long as you have good renters.

Profit Potential: $100 to over $2,000 per month.

13. Renting out your RV

Many people have RV's they only use on occasion, so why not rent it out to other people? Sites like Rvshare - https://rvshare.com/ can help facilitate this for you.

Positives: Quick money renting out something you may not be fully using.

Negatives: Expensive upkeep, bad renters.

Cost: 3/5 – Monthly cost of insurance, maintenance, and depreciation could be over $1,000 a month.

Difficulty Level: 1/5 – As long as you have good renters.

Profit Potential: $100 to over $3,000 per month.

14. Advertising space on your car

You can make cash by simply using your car to advertise. This can be facilitated with sites like Carvertise – https://carvertise.com/drivers/

Positives: Quick money.

Negatives: Might be embarrassing for some.

Cost: 1/5 – No extra costs as long as you are not driving more than normal.

Difficulty Level: 1/5 – Not hard at all.

Profit Potential: $350 – $1,500 per campaign (Different time periods and payouts vary).

15. Renting out your bike, surfboard or snowboard

The site Spinlister – https://www.spinlister.com/list allows you to rent out your bikes, surfboards, or snowboards.

Positives: Quick money renting out something you may not be fully using.

Negatives: Bad renters. Damage and wear and tear on your items.

Cost: 1/5 – Other than wear and tear, no costs.

Difficulty Level: 1/5 – As long as you have good renters.

Profit Potential: $20 - $500 per month.

16. Renting out your boat

If you have a boat you are not using that often, you can rent it out with Boatsetter – https://www.boatsetter.com/a/list-boat

Positives: Quick money renting out something you may not be fully using.

Negatives: Expensive upkeep, bad renters.

Cost: 3/5 – Monthly cost of insurance, maintenance, and depreciation could be over $1,000 a month.

Difficulty Level: 1/5 – As long as you have good renters.

Profit Potential: Over $1,500 per month on average.

17. Renting out your high-end fashion to others

Do you have high-end fashion you are not using? You can rent it out to others with Rent My Wardrobe - https://www.rentmywardrobe.com/

Positives: Quick money renting out something you may not be fully using.

Negatives: Bad renters, not suitable for the germophobic, wear and tear on the clothes.

Cost: 2/5 – Wear and tear on the clothes.

Difficulty Level: 1/5 – As long as you have good renters.

Profit Potential: $10 to over $1,000 a month.

18. Renting out your high-end photography equipment

High-end photography equipment can be costly, and people may only need it for a 1-time reason so they look to rent photo equipment. A site called Kitsplit - https://kitsplit.com/ allows you to rent out your high-end photo equipment.

Positives: Quick money renting out something you may not be fully using.

Negatives: Bad renters, wear and tear on the equipment.

Cost: 2/5 – Wear and tear on the expensive equipment.

Difficulty Level: 1/5 – As long as you have good renters.

Profit Potential: $50 to over $1,000 a month.

19. Renting out high-quality baby gear

In between kids, you may not want to sell your high-quality baby gear, and it most likely stays in your storage. You can profit from this dormant gear by renting it out to other parents.

Positives: Quick money renting out something you may not be fully using.

Negatives: Bad renters, not suitable for the germophobic, wear and tear on the gear.

Cost: 2/5 – Wear and tear on the gear.

Difficulty Level: 1/5 – As long as you have good renters.

Profit Potential: $100 to over $1,000 a month.

20. Renting out your extra internet bandwidth

Many people do not use all their internet bandwidth each month, and you can rent it out to others with Packetstream - https://packetstream.io/

Positives: Quick money on something you might be wasting.

Negatives: If you need the bandwidth later, it might be costly.

Cost: 1/5 – This should be a 1 as long as you are not overdoing the bandwidth yourself.

Difficulty Level: 2/5 – Should be very easy once you learn how to navigate the website.

Profit Potential: $1 to $32 a month.

21. General renting sites

There are general sites to rent out different things, including unusual items like drones, costumers, and almost anything you can think of.

There are different sites for this, including the following:

Fatllama – https://fatllama.com/r/marc-ef3e9

Loanables – https://www.loanables.com/

Rentah –https://www.rentah.com/

Positives: Quick money renting out something you may not be fully using.

Negatives: Bad renters, wear and tear.

Cost: 1/5 – Wear and tear of the items.

Difficulty Level: 1/5 – As long as you have good renters.

Profit Potential: $5 to over $3,000 a month.

Chapter 3:

Freelancing
as a Side Hustle

What is Freelancing:

Although many people understand what freelancing is in case, there might be some readers who do not understand what freelancing is, I will explain it.

Freelancing is where an individual provides expertise in a particular discipline for a specific fee associated with that work. This can include landing contacts with one company, doing freelance work for many companies or growing your own freelance business.

Why do Freelancing?

A common question many individuals ask me is why they should go into freelancing. To answer this question, I will explain some great reasons why you should start freelancing.

Freelance can be very lucrative!

Some individuals, when they think of freelancing, think very small and think of a graphic designer who sells their service for under $100 and makes very little revenue. This is a massive mistake, as a freelance business that is sold, scaled, and grown correctly can be a fantastic revenue generator. For example, the same graphic designer who only charged $100 for their service builds their brand and reputation and now sells their service for $1,000. Going from $100 to $1,000 is a massive difference in profits. Also, they grow their freelance practice to having over 100 clients a month instead of having a few clients. Instead of only making a few hundred dollars a month, they now make $100,000 a month as their 100 clients each pay $1,000 a month.

Obviously, much hard work is needed to grow a freelance practice, but realistically speaking, this is possible if you systematically follow the instructions in this book.

Very little start-up costs

The great thing about starting to freelance is that there are very little start-up costs, as you are selling your knowledge in most cases instead of selling a product. To begin with, for the most part, you just need to have a phone and computer, which the majority of people already have in their homes. This is a super low-cost start-up compared to most businesses.

Freelancing can be done from anywhere

The great thing about starting to freelance is it can be started anywhere in the world, and you can work from almost any location. With modern technology, you can have a phone number associated with the region you are freelancing in, as well as doing calls via Zoom and location is not an issue. Think of working in a tropical paradise or anywhere on the globe you choose. I have friends that have successfully built their freelance businesses and live on tropical islands with low cost of living.

Freelancing can start as a side hustle

The great thing about freelance is that it can be started as a part-time side hustle, and you do not have to give up your day job. As long as your full-time job allows for doing a side hustle, you can start building your freelance practice to a certain level before quitting your day job.

Get paid for something you already have a skill in

Many of us have some type of useful skill that is in demand and yet do not try to profit from these skills. If you have a talent in demand, why not use it to the maximum level to profit from it?

Easy ramp-up time

Freelance can literally start the day you want to start running your freelance firm. It is also easy to scale and grow your own freelance business. Many people think of just a one person freelance firm, but a freelance firm can grow to become a massive enterprise.

How to choose your freelancing discipline

The most important thing you need to do in starting to freelance is to choose your freelance discipline. This might seem obvious, but if you choose the wrong business to do freelance for, you will not be successful.

Freelance in a service you already are an expert in

If possible, choose a freelance business you are already an expert in. In your working career, you must have obtained some specific skills that others do not possess that others would be willing to pay for. An example might be someone with tax experience building a bookkeeper freelance practice. Using your existing expertise would be the most logical place to build a freelance firm from.

There must be a market for that skill

You might have a great skill like underwater basket weaving, but if there is no market for this skill, no one will be interested in your skill. This is why it is important to research ahead of time if there is a market. You do this by simply going onto Google and typing in the skill you would like to market and see if there are many other people doing freelance in this space. Also, visit freelance sites like Fiverr and see if many people are selling the kind of skills you have experience in.

100+ ideas for different freelancing side hustles

I am going to give you a broad idea of different freelance business ideas to choose from. This will be a long list of over a 100, and there are probably hundreds of other freelance side hustle ideas I am forgetting. To make it easy to follow, I will list the ideas in alphabetical order.

List of freelance businesses

Accounting/Finance

1. Accountant
2. Bookkeeper
3. ERP Management
4. Financial Consultant
5. Payroll Consultant
6. Tax Consultant

Architecture & Building Design

1. 3D Architecture
2. 3D Landscape
3. Architecture & Interior Design
4. Landscape Design
5. Building Engineering
6. Building Information Modeling

Arts and Graphics

1. 3D Design
2. 3D Fashion & Garment
3. 3D Industrial Design
4. 3D Jewelry Design
5. AI Artists
6. Album Cover Design
7. Animator
8. Animated GIFs
9. Animation Explainers
10. Animations for Kids
11. Animation for Streamers
12. Art Director
13. Banner/Ad Designer
14. Book Design
15. Book Covers
16. Brand Style Guides
17. Brochure Design
18. Business Cards & Stationery
19. Car Wraps

20. Card Designer
21. Cartoons & Comics
22. Catalog Design
23. Character Animation
24. Character Modeling
25. Children's Book Illustration
26. Email Design
27. Fashion Design
28. Flyer Design
29. Fonts & Typography
30. Game Art
31. Graphic Designer
32. Graphics for Streamers
33. Icon Design
34. Illustrator
35. Image Editing
36. Industrial & Product Design
37. Infographic Designer
38. Invitation Design
39. Interior Designer
40. Jewelry Design
41. Landing Page Design
42. Logo Animation
43. Logo & Brand Identity
44. Logo Design
45. Lottie & Web Animation
46. Marketing Design
47. Menu Design
48. NFT Art
49. Packaging & Covers
50. Packaging & Label Design
51. Pattern Design
52. Photographer
53. Portraits & Caricatures
54. Presentation Design
55. Print Design
56. Podcast Cover Art
57. Poster Design
58. Resume Design
59. Signage Design
60. Social Media Design
61. Story Boards
62. Tattoo Design

63. Thumbnails Design
64. T-Shirts & Merchandise Design
65. Twitch Store
66. Trade Booth Design
67. UI Consultant
68. UX Consultant
69. Vector Tracing
70. Video Editor
71. Videographer
72. Web & App Design
73. Web Banners
74. Website Design

Business Operations

1. Business Coach
2. Business Consultant
3. Business Plans
4. Business Registration
5. Business Strategy Consultant
6. Compliance Consultant
7. e-Commerce Management
8. Logistics Consultant
9. Management Consultant
10. Operations Consultant
11. Payment Gateway Consultant
12. Process Improvement Consulting
13. Researcher
14. Risk Management Consultant
15. Small Business Consultant
16. Six Sigma Consulting
17. Startup Consulting
18. Supply Chain Consultant
19. Training Consultant
20. Virtual Assistant

Engineering Consultant

1. CAD Designer
2. Engineering Consultant
3. Environmental Consultant

HR

1. Benefits Consultant
2. Career Coaching Consultant
3. Compensation Consultant
4. Leave of Absence Consultant
5. HR Consultant
6. Interviewing Consulting
7. Recruitment Consultant
8. Retention Consultant
9. Sourcing Consultant
10. Wellness Consultant

Legal

1. Applications & Registrations
2. Legal Contracts
3. Legal Consultants
4. Legal Writer

Marketing

1. Affiliate Marketing
2. Brand Consultant
3. Book and eBook Marketing
4. Communications Consultant
5. CMS Consultant
6. Direct Mail Consulting

7. Digital Marketer
8. Display Advertising
9. E-Commerce Marketing
10. Email Marketing Consultant
11. Event Manager
12. Guest Posting
13. Influencer Marketing
14. Market Research
15. Marketing Advice
16. Marketing Strategy
17. Media Buyer
18. Methods & Techniques
19. Mobile App Marketing
20. Music Promotion
21. Paid Social Media
22. Pitch Decks
23. Podcast Marketing
24. PR Consultant
25. SEM Consultant
26. SEO Consultant
27. Shopify Consultant
28. Social Media
29. Text Message Marketing
30. Video Marketing
31. Web Analytics

Media & Production

1. App & Website Previews
2. Article to Video
3. Book Trailers
4. Corporate Videos
5. Crowdfunding Videos
6. Editing & Post-Production
7. e-commerce Product Videos
8. eLearning Video Production
9. Film Video Production

10. Game Trailers
11. Intro & Outro Videos
12. Live Action Explainers
13. Meditation Videos
14. Music Videos
15. NFT Animation
16. Real Estate Promos
17. Rigging
18. Screen Casting Video
19. Slideshow Videos
20. Social Media Videos
21. Spokesperson Video
22. Subtitles & Captions
23. UGC Video
24. Video Advice
25. Video Ads & Commercials
26. Video Art
27. Video Editing
28. Video Templates Editing
29. Video Transfer and Conversion
30. Visual Effects
31. YouTube Consultant

Music Production & Writing

1. Audio Ads Production
2. Audio Editing
3. Audio Logic & Sonic Branding
4. Audiobook Production
5. DJ Drops & Tags
6. DJ Mixing
7. Beat Making
8. Jingles & Intros
9. Meditation Music
10. Mixing & Mastering
11. Music & Audio Advice
12. Music Transcription
13. Podcast Production
14. Producers & Composers
15. Remixing & Mashups

16. Singers & Vocalists
17. Session Musicians
18. Songwriters
19. Sound Design
20. Synth Presets
21. Vocal Tuning
22. Voice Over
23. Voice Synthesis & AI

Sales Related

1. Call Center & Calling
2. Crowd Funding
3. Customer Care
4. Franchise Consultant
5. Fundraising Consultant
6. Lead Generator
7. Name Generator
8. Proposal Consultant
9. Sales Consultant
10. Sales Funnel Consultant

Technology

1. AI Consultant
2. App Developer
3. Blockchain & Cryptocurrency
4. Book Formatter
5. Business Analyst Consultant
6. Chatbot Development
7. Cloud Consultant
8. Convert Files
9. CRM Specialist
10. Custom Websites
11. Cybersecurity
12. Data Analyst
13. Database Consultant
14. Desktop Applications
15. DevOps & Cloud
16. Development for Streamers
17. Game Development
18. HRIS consultant

19. IT consultant
20. IT Security consultant
21. Network Analyst
22. NFT Development
23. Project Manager
24. QA Consultant
25. Software Development Consultant
26. Salesforce Consultant
27. Scrum Master

28. Shopify
29. Support & IT
30. User Testing
31. Web Designer
32. Webflow
33. Wix
34. Website Maintenance
35. Website Customization
36. Website Platforms
37. WordPress

Writing/Editing

1. Ad Copy
2. AI Content Writer
3. Articles & Blog Posts
4. Beta Reading
5. Book & eBook Writing
6. Book Editor
7. Brand Voice & Tone
8. Business & Marketing Copy

9. Business Names & Slogans
10. Case Studies
11. Content Strategist
12. Content Writer
13. Copywriter
14. Cover Letters
15. Creative Writing
16. Editor
17. Email Copy
18. Grant Writer

19. Job Descriptions
20. LinkedIn Profile Writer
21. Podcast Writing
22. Press Release Writer
23. Product Descriptions
24. Proofreader
25. Resume Writer
26. Sales Copy
27. Scriptwriting
28. Social Media Copy
29. Speechwriting
30. Summaries
31. Technical Writer
32. Transcriber
33. Translator
34. UX Writer
35. Web Content Writer
36. White Papers
37. Writing Advice

No skills – you can always learn one

If you have no skills to freelance, you can always learn a new skill. Many skills can be learned today online by taking classes on Udemy or even taking a class in community college.

Again, you should pick a subject that both interests you, and there is a market for.

Setting prices for your freelancing services

Not knowing your net value as a freelancer could result in a freelancer being underpaid or overpriced in their market. Deciding what you are going to charge for your freelancing service will depend on many factors such as experience, reputation, location, and, most of all, what your competitors are doing. This chapter will give you insight into setting prices for your freelancing services.

The first step is to know your value

Before setting your freelancing fees, you must know your true value in the marketplace. It would help if you found out what your peers are making at similar freelancing roles for your years of experience. A good site that may help you is Glassdoor, which provides many different firms' salary levels.

Ask peers and people in your industry

Another great way to learn about setting your freelancing price is to ask people you know in your industry. My advice is to ask as many people as possible to learn what the going rate is for someone with your experience.

Understand what the client can afford

You also need to understand what the client you are potentially working with can afford. You might think you are worth a certain amount, but it might be more or less than what the company is looking to pay. Again, checking on Glassdoor or doing research online to find out what past executives have made can give you a good answer.

Demonstrate your value during meetings

Not only should you do an excellent job during the meeting process, but you must be able to sell them on how you can help them achieve success with you as a freelancer. The more value you can demonstrate, the more they will like you and the more room you will have to negotiate.

As you build a reputation, your value will increase

If you continuously deliver in your projects and build your brand as an expert in your field, in time you will be able to charge higher fees for your freelancing engagements.

Keep your word

An essential rule for life is to be honest. If you give a number in terms of fees and then change it during the negotiations, you will be viewed as dishonest and could lose the offer with the client.

Don't delay accepting an offer you like

As soon as you get an offer you like, you should accept it without delay. Do not play hard to get.

If you play games at this stage, a client might withdraw the offer.

Rating Freelancing overview, rating, and profit potential

Positives: Can be a very lucrative side hustle, expandable to full-time work, and has low start-up costs.

Negatives: Takes time to build up clients, and hustling for clients can be time-consuming.

Cost: 1/5 – For most freelancing roles, just a computer and phone. Some freelance roles in media will require expensive equipment if you do not have them.

Difficulty Level: 1/1to5 – If you have an existing skill, it will be a 1/5. If you acquire the needed skill, it can be a 5/5. Also, for some, hustling for business might make it a 5/5. In the next chapter, I will explain that hustling for clients is not hard and can be a 1/5 for difficulty.

Profit Potential: $10 to over $100,000 a month. If you work hard hustling for business, $8,000 a month is very realistic.

Chapter 4:

How to find Freelance Gigs

Asking existing contacts for freelance business

A great source for potential freelance clients is your existing contacts. I can tell you that this has been my number one source for obtaining clients over the years. Think of this in your career of working in a particular space—you have most likely worked with people who know your value already. It is simple to go to these individuals first when starting your quest for freelance work. In my years of freelancing, this has been a regular over 6-figure source of income for me year in and year out. The best part of this business was that it was the easiest to obtain as the contacts knew my work, and it was easy to close.

Think of all your past places of employment

To start, think of all the places you have worked and make a list of all the places you made a contribution. From there, approach leaders you had a good relationship with. Tell them you have started your own freelance firm and tell them about your services. Some might need your services right away or will keep you in mind when they need someone with your skill set. My advice is to follow up with those who do not have any current needs. When they do have a need for your service, you should be on top of that list, especially if you are in regular contact with them.

Think of people you know who could have a need for your freelance services

Most people know of people they do not work with but are in a position to hire someone with your particular skill set. Think of friends and family who might own companies or are managers for companies. Make a list of all these contacts and start contacting these individuals. Tell them directly you have started your freelance business. People trust people they know and will be more likely to hire you as a freelancer as opposed to a stranger.

Finding freelance roles on freelance sites

There has never been a time in history when finding freelance gigs was made easier due to the advent of freelance sites dedicated to finding freelance gigs. Despite the ease of these sites, you have to learn how to master using the most common freelance sites.

Fiverr

I have been using Fiverr for close to 10 years and can tell it is a fantastic way to obtain freelance clients. Despite this, many people view Fiverr and other freelance sites as a place for low-level gigs or feel it is too crowded of a medium. This is not the case, and I can tell you I regularly make $5,000 US a month just off the Fiverr platform alone and now have a team that runs my Fiverr gigs on my behalf. I am not the exception, as some people make 6 figures and the top make 7 figures of this platform alone. Please note: Fiverr takes a 20% cut of your fees, but this is well worth the profit you will obtain from the platform.

So how do some people make little, and others do well on Fiverr? From my experience, there are effective ways to do Fiverr the right way, and below, you will learn this in more detail.

Become a Fiverr Pro

A Fiverr Pro on Fiverr is a section where verified experts have their own area, and many people will search under this section to ensure they work with an expert. In addition, Fiverr Pros usually charge much more than regular Fiverr freelancers. Also, there is less competition, so potential customers will find you much easier than regularly searching on Fiverr.

How to Become a Fiverr Pro

To become a Fiverr Pro, you fill out an application on Fiverr that goes over your work history that qualifies you are an expert. Take the time to do this right if you get accepted; it is almost impossible not to succeed with Fiverr. After making your application, Fiverr does a review process and then conducts an interview with you to determine if you are a match for them. Not all types of consulting gigs are offered at the pro level, so you will have to see if your skill is a match.

You must build your referrals on Fiverr.

There are many people on Fiverr, and if you do not have reviews, people will ignore you, thinking you are not a qualified consultant. What I recommend is to charge a super low price for your service first, building reviews for your service. Once you get 10 reviews, you can raise your rates. In the short term, the sacrifice of low fees will be worth garnering the future cash flow you will build.

Build a well-written Fiverr profile

Just like any landing page, you must execute an effective copy on Fiverr that will make a potential client interested in your Fiverr profile. Fiverr has many sections for you to fill out, and my advice is to take the time and write great copy in these sections. If you are not a good writer, you can outsource this to someone who can write sales copy.

Use images and videos on Fiverr

If you really want to stand out on Fiverr, you must have professional photos and videos that sell your freelance services. When potential clients see high-quality videos about you and their service, their trust level goes up, and you will make more sales. I can tell you that many clients have told me they chose my service on Fiverr due to the video they saw. In addition to videos, make sure you have quality logo photos on your Fiverr page that can sell your service. If you can not make your own logo photos and videos, you can outsource this to a professional who can do a good job for you.

You must have exceptional live customer service on Fiverr

Another thing I recommend is providing exceptional live customer service to clients, especially if you are charging a higher freelance rate. This includes responding quickly to enquiries, if possible, have live meetings, and finish your projects on time and correctly. As you grow and get busy, you may not have time to respond to clients, so I recommend that if you get that big to hire someone to handle this for you.

See my own Fiverr business page.

If you would like more information on Fiverr, for example, please see my own Fiverr page for more information: https://www.fiverr.com/mostynbooks.

Other Freelance sites

There are many other freelance sites, each with both positives and negatives. Depending on your time, you can look for freelance gigs on these sites. Below is a list of some of the bigger sites, and they all have different charges. My advice is to sign up for many with a focus on Fiverr.

Upwork

I have used Upwork, and there is definitely value in using this platform to find freelance gigs.

Just like Fiverr, a wide variety of types of gigs are listed. The difference with this platform compared to Fiverr is the opportunity to bid on gigs posted by potential clients. In the beginning, just to promote your name and reputation, bid low to get gigs to build up your reviews.

Topatal

Topatal is another great freelance site that focuses on skills in the technology domain.

Perspective freelancers apply to be a freelancer, and if accepted, there is less freelance competition than other freelance sites. My advice when applying with Topatal is to ensure you follow their application instructions carefully.

Guru

Guru works similar to Upwork where potential clients post work and freelancers bit on work.

Like other freelance sites, Guru can be crowded with freelancers, so make sure you get reviews and have great content.

There are many freelance sites

There are many other freelance sites out there, and my advice is to do your research and check for reviews on the sites to ensure they are ethical to work with.

Use job boards to find Freelance roles

A logical place many freelancers ignore when searching for freelance roles is simply looking at the many job boards and applying for freelance contracts that match their skill sets. Below I will provide you with information on how to look for freelance roles and a list of many of the major job boards.

Job boards introduction

One of the most common places you will search for a job is on a job board. A job board is a website where employers post roles that need to be filled. Job boards can vary in size from large boards like Indeed to niche boards like Dice, an IT job board. There are also hundreds of smaller boards, including regional boards and boards in almost every job sector. Related to job boards are aggregators, indexed job sites such as Indeed and Glassdoor, which take jobs from many sources and put them in one place.

The importance of speed

An overlooked part of applying for freelance jobs is speed. Every day you delay applying for a job, another person applies for that same job. Before you know it, the employer has enough candidates and closes the job. You have missed out. Employers do not wait for latecomers to submit applications. Usually, the first people to apply have the greatest chance of getting roles. It is common practice for employers to close roles when they have enough candidates in their pipeline. To ensure you are on the top of the list, apply to roles as soon as you see them open.

Delaying by even a few hours is bad enough, but waiting days could cost you that potential job opportunity. How do you find jobs before others do? Sign up for job alerts. Make sure that you check for new job postings every day.

Job alerts

One of the biggest ways a job seeker can save time in their job search is to create job alerts. Job alerts are daily or weekly emails that are sent to job seekers to inform them about open jobs. The job seeker simply signs up for alerts based on the jobs they are interested in.

Quick apply applications

Another great way to save time in your job search is to use quick apply applications. This great tool gives job seekers the option of applying for jobs with a few easy clicks of the mouse.

On most major sites, you are given the option to quick apply for some jobs. What these sites cleverly have done is allow you to apply to jobs with the existing resume or profile you have created. In the case of Indeed and LinkedIn, the job list tells you what jobs offer the quick apply process. A job seeker can save tons of time by applying to many jobs with one easy quick apply process.

Post your resume on all major job boards

It is highly recommended that you post your resume on all the major job boards with all your skills as recruiters and headhunters will be able to find you and present freelance work for you.

List of major job board sites

1. Indeed - http://www.indeed.com/ - More jobs than any other site; remember to include your resume in their database

2. LinkedIn - https://www.linkedin.com/ - Lots of Quick apply

3. ZipRecruiter - https://www.ziprecruiter.com/ - Lots of Quick apply; less competition

4. Glassdoor - https://www.glassdoor.com - Lots of Quick apply

Using staffing firms to find Freelance gigs

Many freelancers talk about the mystical hidden job market as if it is some far-off land like Atlantis. The truth is, there is a hidden job market that many freelancers/job seekers ignore:

agency recruiters. Many companies use recruitment agencies when filling freelance roles so as not to have these freelancers on their payrolls.

For some roles, recruiters have the exclusive domain of recruiting for these freelance jobs. If you are not connected to that recruiter's job, you will not be able to apply to it. With many jobs in the market under agency recruiters' control, it is paramount that you make connections with them. Only then will you be able to apply for those jobs.

One final point about working with agency recruiters: you do not pay a cent to them if you get hired. Agency recruitment firms get paid by the company that hires you—on average, about 20%

markup on your freelance fee. So if you charge $100 an hour, the agency will charge the client $120 an hour. Avoid any recruitment agency that tries to charge you a fee; they are most likely scamming you. In addition, there is no such thing as one recruiter having exclusivity. In fact, it is recommended that you have multiple recruiters. Having multiple recruiters working for you will increase your odds of finding a freelance job since each recruiter could have a separate set of clients.

Think like a recruiter when building your resume

Most recruiters search by keywords when looking to fill roles. Why? Most recruiters are not experts or even very knowledgeable in the field that they are recruiting for. Usually, they go by the titles and keywords that have been given to them by hiring managers. Therefore, when you are writing your resume, try to think like a recruiter. Ask yourself: if I was a recruiter, what would I be looking for in a resume? Make sure to use the most commonly known term for your job title. Improve SEO by mentioning your job title whenever possible (without being overly repetitive). Insert as many keywords into your resume as you can.

How to connect with recruiters

1. Search on LinkedIn.

Making connections with recruiters is an effective way to expand your job search. Below you will find ways to connect with recruiters.

Connect with recruiters on LinkedIn. To do this, go to https://www.linkedin.com/. In the search bar, enter the industry you work in and the word recruiter (for example: technology recruiter).

Profiles of recruiters who specialize in your profession will pop up. To connect with a recruiter, click the Connect button next to their picture. After they accept your request, send them an email stating that you are looking for a job. Almost all recruiters will accept your invite request.

2. Research agency recruiters in your industry

One way to do this is by Google search: in the search box, type "recruitment agency" and the industry you are looking for. Once you have a list of agencies to contact, send each your resume and, if possible, try to connect with them via phone. Not all recruiters will get back to you.

Nonetheless, those who do will be able to open doors for you.

3. Ask your current and former colleagues for recruiter referrals

A great way to connect with recruiters is to ask current and former colleagues for referrals of good recruiters they have worked with.

4. Apply for jobs that agencies have posted

Find agency recruiters by applying for jobs that agencies have posted. If you are qualified for roles presented by the recruiter, there is a good chance the recruiter will contact you.

Finding and cold-calling companies

The most challenging way to grow your freelance business is finding new business and seeking out that business directly. Nonetheless, it is an important skill to learn to expand your client base.

For many freelancers, this is one of the hardest things to do. The ability to speak to a potential client outside of the blue and convince them to be interested in your freelance service is truly an art form. This section will teach you how to find new business. In addition, it will teach you how to be confident in making phone calls and providing techniques to cold call potential new clients.

How to find new clients

When looking for new potential clients, think of a business that could use your potential skill.

For example, if you provide bookkeeping services for small businesses, research local small businesses and then go on LinkedIn to see who the owner of the small business is, then look up the business number and call them directly. If you have a more specialty skill that a big to medium size company could use, such as software development, look up companies you would want to work for on LinkedIn and look up who the Software

Development manager is. This is easy to do as you only need to type in the company and the title you are looking for on LinkedIn, and it should list the right contact for you. From there, you can either send the person a LinkedIn message, email them, or call them for their business.

Overcome your cold-calling fears

For many freelancers, calling an individual out of the blue and trying to solicit them for work is a traumatic thought. Learning to overcome these fears will make cold calling a more pleasant experience. This will translate into long-term success for you as a freelancer. Below you will find tips to overcome your cold-calling fears:

It's just people

Why be scared of calling someone? Remember: the people you are calling are just people. They eat, sleep and make mistakes just like you, so do not be afraid of them.

Always think we are doing the potential client a favor

Just think that when you are cold-calling, you are going to be presenting someone who can fulfill a freelance need they have and doing them a favor. Logically speaking, most people are interested in someone who can fulfill a need for them.

Overcome rejection

Rejection is a fact with cold-calling, as only about 1% of clients will be interested in you. Ninety-nine percent of clients will not be interested, so do not take it personally.

Practice makes perfect

The old saying is true. This also applies to making cold calls. The more calls you make, the better and more comfortable you will be at it. My first sales manager made me practice cold-calling over and over again. It was hard work, but now it's as easy for me as riding a bike.

Don't procrastinate

Never procrastinate when making cold calls. This type of behavior will set you up for failure, as you will becoming increasingly hesitant to call as time goes on.

Positive motivation

Think of the reason you are making the cold calls, and that is to be successful at your job as well as potential remuneration.

Avoid negative thoughts

Do not let negative thoughts betray you in terms of what can go wrong. When you make your cold calls, relax and try not to worry.

Role play

Try practicing with your friends and on your own. Sometimes practicing your pitch with people before talking to strangers can make you more comfortable.

Have realistic expectations

On average, only 1% of people contacted via a cold call are interested. You can never be 100% with cold calls, so having realistic expectations can make you feel good.

Hands-on coaching

A technique I have used with freelancers is first to have them listen to 3-5 of my cold calls. Then I listen to 3-5 of their calls and give them feedback. From there, they listen to 3-5 more of my cold calls. Then I listen to 3-5 more of their calls and provide more feedback. Finally, the freelancer is ready to make calls on their own. This technique helps the freelancer become comfortable.

Engage clients through voice messages

In many cases, when reaching out to a potential client via phone, you will not get a live person.

That being the case, you can still leave a voice message as a form of engaging with clients. Many people do not leave voice messages. In the process, they miss a great opportunity to engage with clients. Below you will find to create effective voice messages that will engage prospective clients.

Step 1: Introduction

Your first sentence should briefly explain who you are. Mention your name and the nature of the call which is to provide freelance services.

Step 2: Sell them on your skills

Your second sentence is the most important sentence—as you have to quickly sell them on your skills.

Step 3: Call to action

Your final sentence should tell the potential clients how to contact you back or by replying to an email you are going to send them.

Other voice message tips

1. Keep the voice message short.

2. Sound professional and not casual.

3. Make sure to speak slowly and ensure that your words are clear, especially when leaving your contact information.

4. Be clear about who you are. If the prospect understands that you are a real person, they will be more likely to call you back.

5. Do not sound like a used car salesman, as clients will most likely not call you back.

Putting it all together—Example Script leaving a voice message for a client

Hi, Dave, my name is Steve Mostyn. I'm a recruitment consultant, and I was wondering if you have any openings on your team for a recruitment consultant? I have over 10 years of recruitment consulting experience working for your local competitors with excellent references.

Feel free to please call me back at 416-111-1111. Alternatively, I sent you a detailed email. If you are interested in learning more, please let me know a good time to speak. Thank you for your time and have a great day.

Using LinkedIn to find Freelance Business

Another great value-added tool is to use LinkedIn to find and connect with potential leads. This section will explain how to find and connect with potential leads.

Step 1: Research for leads

Looking for leads is relatively easy on LinkedIn as all you need to do is type in the search bar on the top of LinkedIn for potential companies you are looking to sell to and type in the person at that company that you most likely would sell to.

An example would be if you want to sell to a CIO at Bank of America, you will type that in the search bar, and that person should pop up.

Step 2: Connect with that lead

Connect with that lead by sending them an invitation to connect.

Step 3: Message the lead

This is where most people fail by aggressively sending the lead a message right away. A better option would be to take your time and interact with the person on LinkedIn or give them something of value, like sharing industry intel. Over time, once you have developed a relationship, you can solicit them with your potential offerings.

How to create a LinkedIn Business Landing Page

In order for potential clients to value you as a freelancer, I recommend building a LinkedIn business landing page. This section will detail how to create a LinkedIn business page from scratch, step by step.

Why build a LinkedIn Business Page

Before I explain how to build a LinkedIn business page, I want to explain why you should have a LinkedIn business page if you own a business or service.

Just like people search LinkedIn to see what they do, they will search to see if you have a LinkedIn business page. If they do not see one, they will think less of you and your business.

On the other hand, if you have a LinkedIn business page, and it looks unprofessional to potential clients, they will view you as unprofessional.

In addition, if you do not have a LinkedIn business page, your LinkedIn profile will not have a visual picture of the logo of your business under your work experience at your firm.

Steps in building a LinkedIn Business Page

Step 1:

On your personal LinkedIn page, click the Work Icon.

Step 2:

Scroll to the bottom and click Create a Company Page.

Step 3:

On the Create a LinkedIn Page, click Company.

Step 4:

This brings you to a page where you fill out details on your business, including the following below.

Name

For this section, you fill in the name of your company.

Linkedin.com/company/

For this section, you create a custom LinkedIn URI. For this, I recommend, if possible,   make a URI that is your business name.

Website

For this section, you list your company website if you have one.

Industry

For this section, you write your industry.

Organization size

For this section, you use the drop-down to select the size of your organization.

Organization type

For this section, you use the drop-down to find and select your organization type.

Logo

For this section, you upload your company logo. If you do not have one, I recommend getting one made.

Tagline

For this section, you write a 120-charter space about your business.

Verification checkmark

For this section, you checkmark to verify the business belongs to you.

Step 5:

You are brought to the admin page to finish adding info on your business. Look for the following sections below on the page to add information:

Description

After selecting this section will bring you to a page where you can add a complete description of your business. Also, your phone number, year founded, and up to 20 keywords that will help customers find you. Also, on the left side of the description, you can look for sections to add things like Location.

Example of my own LinkedIn Business Page

Below you will find info on my LinkedIn business page, or feel free to check it out at this link:

https://www.linkedin.com/company/68173296/admin/

Company

Career Boost Group

Website

https://careerboostgroup.com/

Industry

Human Resources

Organization size

201-500 employees

Organization type

Privately held

Tagline

The largest privately held integrated Career & HR Consulting Service Human Resources New York, NY

Description

Career Boost is the largest privately held integrated Career & HR Consulting Service. Career Boost's many different subsidiaries and brands allow many ways for both individuals and organizations to receive the highest level of both Career and HR consulting and training.

Location

New York, NY

Specialties

HR, Human Resources, Recruitment, Resume Writing, LinkedIn Profile Writing, Interview Training, CV Writing, RPO, Resume Translation, Outplacement, Executive Search, Recruitment Consulting, Recruitment Training, HR Consulting, Sourcing, Bio Writing, Staffing Agency, Healthcare, Banking, IT, Retained Search, Contingency Search, and Job Search Consulting By following the ideas presented in this section, you will learn how to build a LinkedIn professional page for your business easily.

How to create a Freelance Page on LinkedIn

This new feature on LinkedIn allows the public to find you when they are looking for a freelancer. Below you will find step-by-step suggestions for how to build your freelance page:

Step 1

Just below your headline section is a section titled Providing Services. Click that link.

Step 2

The link will take you to a page to fill out the information on your freelance services. This includes the following sections to fill out.

About

For this section, write a small summary of your service. LinkedIn gives you limited space, so keep the wording within space parameters.

Pricing

If you are comfortable, list the price of your services.

Services provided

List all the different services you offer.

Media

You can upload videos and pictures of your services to add visuals to your freelance profile.

Review

You can send 15 review requests to people on LinkedIn who can review your services.

Do a good job and build your referral network to get more freelance business

One of the best ways to expand your freelance side hustle is to do a good job with your clients. This alone should build your reputation and result in many referrals of people reaching out to you for your help.

Chapter 5:

Selling Your Knowledge Through Digital Products

I n the previous chapters, I wrote about freelancing as a side hustle. To go along with freelancing where you sell your expertise as a service, you can build digital products based on your expertise which can be sold to people looking to expand their knowledge of a particular topic. This can include writing books, and articles, recording a training session or a course.

Digital products have more topics than Freelancing

You would be surprised what non-fiction book or course you can create that people would be interested in. Basically, any topic a person might be interested in you can create a digital product for. For example, things like photography, singing lesson, collectibles, and almost any topic is possible. I would look at different sites and see what might be popular. Also, make sure you know a lot about a topic if you are going to create a digital product of it.

Write books

A possible digital product for you to do as a side hustle is writing books on your expertise areas.

This will require some skill as a writer, but it is easier than you think. I have written over 10 books, and I can tell you, over the years, the point of entry for writing and even publishing books has become easier. You can either go the traditional publisher route or self-publish. The cost to publish on your own has come down, and publishing on Amazon does not cost anything. The only cost will be editing, formatting, and book promotion. Although all these things can be learned. Even book covers can be done reasonably today or for free on Canva.

My book sales every month provide me with a nice royalty check month after month to go along with my many other side hustles. In addition, my books help to promote my services and expand my influence as a leader in my spaces.

95% you will not become rich writing books

Writing and selling books is a great extra way to supplement your income, but almost everyone who writes books does not become rich writing them. They say if you make an income that a minimum wage job earner would earn in total income at the end of the year, then you did well with selling books. On average, you make a percentage of books sold on Amazon. For example, if you sell a digital book for $2.99, you would make close to $2. If you sold a print book for $9.99 you would make close to $3. Obviously, if you charge more, you make more profit but you might sell fewer books. As you can see, it is a small amount of profit for each book sold, but it can add up. If you sell 100 books in a month at $3, that would be an extra $300 in your pocket. Over a year that is an extra $3,600 in income that most likely does not need any more work.

My own experience

Over 100,000+ people have bought or downloaded my many books. I am not saying I am an expert but after over ten books, I have learned some solid things. The one thing

I will say, there is no guarantee when it comes to books. One of the best books I ever wrote was called Job Search:

Fundamentals of Effective Job Hunting, Resumes, and Interviews. This comprehensive book on job hunting was at one time the #1 non-fiction book, but I lost a little bit of money on the book as for some reason, after a few months, it just stopped selling. If I factor in the money I spent on marketing, and the cost of making the book Job Search probably cost me a bit of money overall.

Then other books I wrote, such as Recruiting 101 has been a constant seller for me month in and out for over 7 years with $0 spent ever on marketing on the book. I will say this: I would not continue to write and promote books if the time and money did not result in a profit for me and my family.

Book tips

Step 1: Write a book there is a market for

The most important thing is to write a book people will actually want to buy. To do this, go to Amazon and type in the topic you want to write about. If no one is buying books on that related topic, there is a good chance no one will. This is why I only recommend writing a non-fiction book! My least-selling book of all time was my only none-fiction book, it was a children's book.

Step 2: Write a quality book

It goes without saying if you are going to write a book, you have to make sure it will be well written.

Step 3: Choose a title that people will look for

Maybe the most important thing when writing a book is to choose a title that people will search for on Amazon. Again, go to Amazon and see in your topic what keywords people are searching for. For example, if you write a book on bookkeeping and to be cute and flashy, you call your book "The ways of Numbers in your Business," no one will search for that as opposed to calling your book "Bookkeeping Fundamentals," which more people will search for.

Step 4: Get it professionally edited

If you go through the trouble of writing a book, go the extra mile and get it professionally edited.

I can tell you firsthand that in a few books I wrote, I made the mistake of not using a pro editor, and it cost me a ton of money in book sales.

Costs: If you use a site like Fiverr, you can find Editors from $80 to $300

Step 5: Create or get created a great cover

A cover must be easy to read, not cluttered, and catch the attention of the audience who in most cases will be browsing Amazon.

Costs: If you use a site like Fiverr, you can find a book illustrator from $30 to $300 or learn to do it yourself on sites like Canva or Illustrator.

Step 6: Get your book professionally formatted

Your book at the end of the day must look like a book, so for that I would use a pro book formatter.

Cost: $30 to $300 or learn how to do book formatting for Kindle and Print.

Step 7: Do both eBook and paperback

You wrote a book so you might as well convert it to both Kindle (eBook) and a paperback. This can allow you to have 2 sources of income from 1 book.

Step 8: Uploading and publishing the book on Amazon

Publishing on Amazon will cost you nothing. All you need to do is go to https://kdp.amazon.com/ and follow the easy-to-follow instructions.

Step 9: Pricing your book

My recommendation is to keep your prices low as more people will more likely buy your book if the prices are kept reasonable.

Step 10: Promote the book

In the perfect world, you would write a great book, publish it, sit back, and make money. This is not the case, and you need to promote the book. Most people are not going to have the budget to do massive PR and sales campaigns. I recommend doing a free Kindle countdown on Amazon Kindle as a reasonable promotional idea. This campaign will allow you to make your Kindle book free for 1-5 days. Some of you are probably wondering why I would promote my book for free? The answer is on Amazon when people get your book for free, it still counts as a sale in terms of boosting your ranking, which in turn will make people find your book. For the promotion you will still need to promote the book, and below are some great sites, both paid and free.

Free sites to promote your books

1. http://itswritenow.com/submit-your-book/

2. http://www.icravefreebies.com/free-kindle-book-submission/

3. http://pretty-hot.com/submit-your-book/

4. http://digitalbooktoday.com/

5. https://ohfb.com/book-sale-notice/

6. http://awesomegang.com/submit-your-book/

7. http://www.totallyfreestuff.com/submit.asp

8. http://www.freestufffinder.com/contact-us/

9. https://www.book-circle.com/submit-free-kindle-ebook-listing/

10. https://contentmo.com/submit-your-free-ebook-promo

11. https://freebooktips.com/authors/submit-your-bargain-book

12. https://bestbookmonkey.com

13. https://bookbongo.com/submit/

14. https://www.book-circle.com/submit-free-kindle-ebook-listing/

15. http://discountbookman.com/book-promotion/

16. https://form.jotform.com/21058917419963

17. https://newfreekindlebooks.com/authors/

18. https://readingdeals.com/submit-ebook/free

Paid sites to promote your free books

1. https://www.freebooksy.com/freebooksy-feature-pricing/

2. http://www.thefussylibrarian.com/for-authors/

3. https://robinreads.com/author-signup/

4. http://ereadernewstoday.com/pricing/

Step 11: Reviews

Reviews are important to drive sales to your book. Always ask readers at the end of the book to write you a review if they liked the book.

Writing and publishing book overview

Positives: Can be a very lucrative side hustle, helps to build your brand, you do it once and then receive continuous royalties, and can help sell other products or services.

Negatives: Requires writing skills, can be time-consuming for some, requires some knowledge of book marketing. Potential not to earn anything if you do not market your book the right way or write a bad book. Even still, you can even write the best book, market it well and still not sell any books.

Cost: 2/5 – If you learn how to do things like formatting and covers yourself, it can be a 1. Anywhere from $0 a book to over $1,000 if you do not budget correctly. With the average cost being $150 a book if you budget correctly and if you find good vendors to work with. Marketing costs can be anywhere from free to over $300 a book.

Difficulty Level: 4-5 – If you do not have writing skills, writing a book will be a hard thing to do. Also requires knowledge of the Amazon platform, Book marketing. Also, knowledge of book covers, editing, and book formatting either to do yourself or outsource.

Profit Potential: $0 to $10,000+ a month, depending on how many books you write. The average for a writer with a few good books would be over $1,000 a month.

Make and sell courses in your area of expertise

Selling courses in your area of expertise is another possible revenue generator. You can sell pre-recorded courses/classes on sites like Udemy. Not only can you make extra revenue, but it will also expand your brand as an expert in your field.

How it works

Just like writing a book, you can record a class or course on many sites that give you a percentage of the payment that people ordering the class pay to the course site. Also, each platform has different charges anywhere from free to hundreds of dollars. So some sites might have more risk.

Steps to writing a class or course

Step 1: Pick a topic that people are looking to learn

See on the various course sites what classes are popular to give you an idea of what classes or courses might sell.

Step 2: Write a script and course

Write a script that should allow you to do at least a 1-hour course.

Step 3: Record the course

Use a high-quality camera and microphone to record the course.

Step 4: Edit the class or course

Use decent editing software to edit the course.

Step 5: Upload the class or course to many learning sites

Upload the class/course to as many learning sites as possible such as the following:

Udemy – https://www.udemy.com/

Skillshare – https://www.skillshare.com/en/

Teachable – https://teachable.com/

Thinkific – https://www.thinkific.com/pricing/

Coursera – https://www.coursera.org/

Plus many more!

Step 6: Market the class or course

Post the class on social media, to your contacts, or create ads on social media.

Positives: Can be a very lucrative side hustle, helps to build your brand, you do it once and then receive continuous royalties, and can help sell other products or services.

Negatives: Requires presentation and recording skills, can be time-consuming for some, and requires some knowledge of broadcasting. Potential not to earn anything if you do not market your course the right way or record a bad course.

Cost: 2/5 – If you do not have a proper camera and recording equipment and recording software you will have an upstart cost of $500 - $2,000 dollars. Also, some platforms can charge a big fee to host and promote your courses. And it could be expensive to market your courses.

Difficulty Level: 3-5 – If you do not have presentation skills or fail to learn to use broadcasting/editing software, it could be difficult.

Profit Potential: $0 to $1,000+ a month, depending on how many courses you do. The average for many is a few hundred dollars a month.

Chapter 6:

Dumpster Diving for Profits

Some of the best things in life are free, and the same with these side hustles I am about to explain. Although free, these side hustles might not be for all due to the nature of the gigs, but I can tell you firsthand that there are decent profits with these side gigs.

Selling items you find in the trash

Every week across most of the world, people and businesses throw away valuable items they deem as trash. Many things, in fact, get thrown away, including furniture, toys, collectibles, books, and even valuable antiques. Just about any week on garbage day, you can find many potential valuable items left outside for the garbage people to pick up and thrown away forever.

My own experience

At one point in my life, when I needed quick cash, I did this for a bit of time and made myself over $1,000 a month in profit.

This side hustle is not for Germaphobes or people who get embarrassed easily!

If germs bug you, do not attempt this side hustle, as you have to literally go into people's garbage and pick things up. In addition, if you get embarrassed easily, this side hustle will not be for you as you have to pick up other people's trash.

What items to look for

Below is a noncomplete list of what items can have value to sell. Also, look to make sure the items are not broken and not unsellable. It will take some time to learn what items to sell, and you can look on eBay and local classified sites to see what items people want to buy from you.

1. Antiques
2. Bikes
3. Books
4. Clothes
5. Collectibles
6. Computers
7. Furniture
8. Garden Tools
9. Gym Equipment
10. Home Décor

11. Jewelry
12. Kitchen Items
13. Luggage
14. Musical Instruments
15. Purses
16. Scooters
17. Shoes
18. Sporting Goods
19. Textbooks
20. Tools
21. Toys
22. Used Appliances
23. Used Car Parts
24. Used Electronics
25. Wheelchairs

When to look

Obviously, the best day to look is on garbage day, but the truth is almost any day of the week people and businesses throw things onto their curve or dumpsters.

Etiquette of dumpster diving

Yes, there is an etiquette to dumpster diving, as many people and especially businesses do not like trespassers on their property. I used to knock on their door to get their permission before removing the item.

Cleaning and fixing items

Before selling the item to get the maximum value, it is recommended that you clean and fix all items.

Where to sell the items

There are many places you can sell your item, and below is a list. Also, it may take time to learn what site will generate you the most profit. In addition, some sites will require you to sell the item in person. When meeting in person always keep security in mind.

1. Amazon – https://www.amazon.com/

2. Bonanza – https://www.bonanza.com/

3. Craigslist – https://www.craigslist.org/about/sites

4. Ebay – http://www.ebay.com/

5. Esty – https://www.etsy.com/

6. Facebook Marketplace – https://www.facebook.com/marketplace/

7. Gazelle (electronics) – https://www.gazelle.com/trade-in

8. Hava a Garage Sale

9. OfferUp – https://offerup.com/

10. Swappa – (electronics) https://swappa.com/

Positives: Easy to do and learn, only cost is gas money.

Negatives: Not for germaphobes or those who get embarrassed easily.

Cost: 1/5 – Only a little bit of gas money.

Difficulty Level: 1-5 beyond easy to learn. Some items might be heavy to pick up and carry.

Profit Potential: $0 to $4,000+ a month, depending on the effort and time you put into it.

Selling cardboard

There are companies, municipalities, and individuals who will pay for cardboard. Below you will learn more about this side hustle.

Where to find cardboard for free?

1. Look at stores that use boxes, like grocery stores, and ask for permission to take boxes.

2. Dumpster dive and get permission for people throwing out clean carboard.

3. Post on local social media groups that you are looking for cardboard.

4. Post on online free classifieds like craigslist that you are looking for cardboard.

5. U-Haul Exchange –
   https://www.uhaul.com/Exchange/ is where you can
   search for people giving away free cardboard boxes.

6. Freecycle – https://www.freecycle.org/ – a site
   where people give away free things such as
   cardboard boxes.

7. Nextdoor.com – check your local area to see if
   anyone is giving away free boxes.

Where to sell cardboard

1. Selling Cardboard to a Recycling Center – This could
   be some municipalities or private companies
   depending on your location.

2. Box Cycle –
   https://www.boxcycle.com/sell_used_boxes – a site
   that buys used boxes.

3. Boxsmart – http://www.boxsmart.net/sell/surplus-
   boxes/ – a site that buys cardboard.

Positives: Make extra money with no skills needed.

Negatives: Lots of work and hustling needed. Can be very
messy.

Cost: 1/5 – Gas money and a car will be required.

Difficulty Level: 1-5 – Super easy to learn.

Profit Potential: It will take a massive volume of cardboard to make money - $1 to over $2 per 100 pounds of loose cardboard.

Selling scarp metal

Just like cardboard you can sell metal for profit as metal is always needed by scrap yards.

Where can I find scrap metal?

Other than your own scrap metal you can find scrap metal that both residence and business throw out. People and businesses throw out scrap metal on their curve and dumpsters. As I have mentioned before I do recommend getting permission before taking anything.

What kind of metal to look for?

1. Aluminum
2. Brass and Bronze
3. Copper
4. Ferrous metals such as cast iron
5. Lead
6. Stainless steel

Where to sell scarp metal

In most locations the best place to scrap metal is scrap yards. I would recommend calling a few to see which one can pay you the most or seem honest. Also check out Beter Business Bureau rating and other review.

Positives: Make extra money with no skills needed.

Negatives: Can be very messy, can be heavy lifting, in some markets can be over saturated.

Cost: 1/5 – Gas money and a car will be required.

Difficulty Level: 3-5 – Once you learn to identify the value of metals and where to sell them it becomes easy. Can be physical and messy.

Profit Potential: Below for each metal you will learn the average dollar per pound value. This will vary also depending on location and the local scrap metal yards are willing to pay.

Aluminum - .30 to over .50 cents a pound Brass - $1.20 to over $2.00 per pound Bronze - $1.20 to over $1.60 per pound Copper - $2.00 to over $4.00 per pound Ferrous Metals such as Cast Iron Lead - .10 to over .90 cents a pound Stainless steel - .10 to over .90 cents a pound

Chapter 7:

Buying and Selling Used Items for Profits

If you were to ask most people at some point in their life, they have sold a used item to another for money. This common side hustle is easy for most people to learn and implement. Below I will provide tips.

My own experience

At one point in my life, I did this part-time and made over $3,000 a month, and I specialized in mostly collectibles.

Start small and then go big!

My advice is to start small, maybe selling your own things and then expanding to buy once you understand what will sell and how much profit you can make from each item.

Start selling in one domain then expand

I recommend learning one item to sell and then expanding to others. I started with collectibles as that was something I knew the value of, then I expanded to other things like books and small electronics, which I learned.

Learn the dollar value of items before you buy them

It is critical before you start buying things to sell to understand what profit you will make from the item. For instance, if you find a board game at Goodwill for $10 but the market for the game is $8-$10, it is not something you would want to buy to sell.

Common items to try to sell

Many of the items in the dumpster diving chapter are listed here, plus many more items.

1. Antiques
2. Art
3. Baby Items
4. Bedding
5. Backpacks
6. Bikes

7. Board games
8. Books
9. Cameras and Video Equipment
10. Cars
11. Clothes
12. Collectibles
13. Computers and Tablets
14. Craft Supplies
15. Furniture
16. Garden Tools
17. Gift Cards
18. Gym Equipment
19. High End Fashion
20. Holliday Decorations
21. Home Décor
22. Jewelry
23. Kitchen Items
24. Luggage
25. Memorabilia
26. Motorcycles
27. Musical Instruments
28. Office Furniture
29. Outdoor Items
30. Party Favors/Decorations
31. Precious Metals
32. Purses
33. Records
34. Recreational vehicles
35. School Supplies
36. Scooters
37. Shoes
38. Smartphones 39. Sporting Goods
40. Textbooks
41. . Tools
42. . Toys
43. . Used Appliances
44. Used Car Parts
45. Used Electronics
46. Vans and Trucks
47. Video Games & Gaming Systems
48. Watches
49. Wedding Accessories
50. Wheelchairs and Crutches

Where to find items

There are many places to look for stuff cheap to buy, which you can then flip into selling for a profit. Below is a good list to look at both in person and online. Finding things all the time is not guaranteed and you have to know what you are looking for and act quickly if you see something selling for a good price.

1. Craigslist – https://www.craigslist.org/about/sites

2. Community Sales

3. Estate Sales

4. Facebook Market Place –
   https://www.facebook.com/marketplace/

5. Flea Markets

6. Garage Sales

7. Goodwill 8.   OfferUp – https://offerup.com/

9. Post ads to find people to sell to you.

10. Thrift stores

Where to sell items

It will not mean anything if you cannot find buyers for the stuff you have bought. Below are some places to sell your items at with many others out there.

1. Amazon - https://www.amazon.com/ - Great for many items but there is a cost to sell but it is the biggest marketplace in the world.

2. Bonanza - https://www.bonanza.com/.

3. Craigslist - https://www.craigslist.org/about/sites - Great place to sell almost anything, you might not get full value.

4. Dealers/Other Sellers – If you want to sell something quickly and you got a good deal on it you can sell it to other sellers or dealers.

5. eBay - http://www.ebay.com/ - Great place to sell many items and one of the largest places to sell used items.

6. Esty - https://www.etsy.com/ - Great place to sell craft and collectibles.

7. Repeat Customers – Develop relationships with your customers to sell them on an ongoing basis. I did this

when I sold collectibles, and it allowed me to sell items faster as I knew things my customers wanted to buy.

8. Gazelle - https://www.gazelle.com/trade-in - Great place to sell electronics.

9. OfferUp - https://offerup.com/ - Great place to sell things fast.

10. Swappa - (electronics) https://swappa.com/- Great place to sell electronics.

Positives: Easy to do and learn.

Negatives: Potential of buying something that will not sell.

Cost: 2/5 – Only a little bit of gas money and the cost to buy items if you start small.

Difficulty Level: 1-5 beyond easy to learn. Some items might be heavy to pick up and carry.

Profit Potential: $0 to $10,000+ a month, depending on if you get good at finding and selling items. Also, on how much effort and time you put into it.

Chapter 8:

Amazon Retail Arbitrage

Amazon Retail Arbitrage is when you find and buy items for sale at other retailers and sell them for a higher price on Amazon. This interesting side hustle made the news a while back when it came to light that some people were making 7 figures doing this.

Steps to doing Amazon Retail Arbitrage

Step 1: Get a membership on Amazon as a seller

Get a paid membership on Amazon as a seller – https://sellercentral.amazon.com/ It will cost you $39.99 a month plus selling fees.

Step 2: Look for sales at your local retailers

Go to your local retailers that can have sales, like grocery chains, dollar stores, and warehouse clubs to look for things that appear discounted.

Step 3: Use a scanning app to determine what the price would be on Amazon

Download a scanning app that will be used to determine if the thing you spot at the retailer is in fact something you can profit from. Below is a list of scanning apps that can be found in most app stores.

A. **Amazon Seller App**

B. **Scoutify**

C. **Profit Bandit**

D. **Scoutly**

E. **ScanPower**

Step 4: Double-checking on Amazon

I recommend double-checking on Amazon to see how things are selling and how much Competition there is. Also, many scanning apps are not perfect, so you should double-check on Amazon.

Step 5: Check reviews

If the product has bad reviews, I would not recommend buying it.

Step 6: Buy the product

If everything checks out, buy the product at the retailer. I recommend starting small and learning and expanding.

Step 7: Post the item on Amazon

Post the item on Amazon and when ordered, follow delivery instructions very carefully to ensure the customer will receive the item.

Positives: Easy to do and learn and can be profitable.

Negatives: Oversaturated market, buying items high and forced to sell low or worse, not being able to sell the item at all. Can be time-consuming not finding things at lower prices than Amazon.

Cost: 2-5/5 – If you start off small and only buy a small amount of merchandise, then this is a 2. If you expand and do this at the industrial level, you will require lots of cash to buy merchandise, and it can be a 5. Also, you will be paying $39.99 a month plus selling fees.

Difficulty Level: 2-5. This is not too hard to learn.

Profit Potential: $0 to $100,000+ a month, depending on how good you get at finding cheap items and reselling in back on Amazon.

Chapter 9:

Drop Shipping Products

Many have heard of drop shipping, and this is where you find on other e-commerce sites like Amazon cheaper products and sell them for a higher price on Amazon or on another e-commerce sites or your own e-commerce store. As Amazon is the easiest to learn, I will be focusing my drop shipping to Amazon.

Step 1: Get a membership on Amazon as a seller

Get a paid membership on Amazon as a seller - https://sellercentral.amazon.com/ It will cost you $39.99 a month plus selling fees.

Step 2: Find items on other e-commerce sites like Amazon

Look through other e-commerce sites for items to sell on Amazon. Look at what other people are selling on Amazon, reviews, and cost of items and what you can sell it for on Amazon. Also, think about shipping costs. In terms of sites, look at the following to find different products to sell.

1.   AliExpress - https://www.aliexpress.us/

2.   Alibaba - https://www.alibaba.com/

3.   DHGate.com - https://www.dhgate.com/

4.   Worldwide Brands - https://www.worldwidebrands.com/

5.   Banggood - https://usa.banggood.com/en

Step 3: Double-checking on Amazon

I recommend double-checking on Amazon to see how things are selling and how much Competition there is.

Step 4: Buy the product

If everything checks out, buy the product. I recommend starting small and learning and expanding.

Step 5: Post the item on Amazon

Post the item on Amazon, and when ordered, follow delivery instructions very carefully to ensure the customer will receive the item.

Positives: Can be profitable.

Negatives: Very oversaturated market, buying items high and being forced to sell low or worse, not being able to sell the item at all. Can be time-consuming not finding things at lower prices than Amazon.

Cost: 2-5/5 – If you start off small and only buy a small amount of merchandise, then this is a 2. If you expand and do this at the industrial level, you will require lots of cash to buy merchandise, and it can be a 5. Also, you will be paying $39.99 a month plus selling fees.

Difficulty Level: 2-5. This is not too hard to learn.

Profit Potential: $0 to $10,000+ a month, depending on how good you get at finding cheap items and reselling in back on Amazon.

Chapter 10:

Drop Shipping Printed Products

Like drop-shipping products for this side hustle, you drop-ship printed items like printed t-shirts. Basically, on a print site you design a T-shirt design then sell it on e-commerce sites like Amazon or Etsy.

Step 1: Sign-up on printing sites to create your printed product such as the following sites

Printify - https://printify.com/how-it-works/

Printful - https://www.printful.com/

SPOD - https://www.spod.com/

Apliiq - https://www.apliiq.com

Step 2: Create a design on a product

Products like T-shirts, Hoodies, Backpacks, Fridge magnets, Cups, Stickers, Swimwear, Skirts, Blankets, and many more.

Step 3: Create a seller page on e-commerce sites

You can create a sellers page on different sites like Amazon, Etsy, or Shopify.

Step 4: Use social media to sell the product

Market the products through social media using paid ads. Be careful with this, as it can be costly.

Positives: Can be profitable.

Negatives: Very oversaturated market, can be time-consuming.

Cost: 2-5/5 – Cost of social media ads. Also, if on Amazon or other sites membership fees. In addition, fees on printing sites.

Difficulty Level: 2-5. The marketing can take some time to learn.

Profit Potential: $0 to $10,000+ a month, depending on how good you are at marketing the items.

Chapter 11:

Selling Digital Artistic Work

Many people have artistic talent in music, photography, and video, and many of these things can be sold as digital products for small but easy cash.

1. Selling photos

Many people need various stock photos for commercial purposes and are willing to pay for stock photos. There are many sites that act as middlemen in helping you sell your photos for commercial purposes. Please note that this side hustle brings a very small return, but cash is cash.

These sites include but are not limited to the following:

https://www.pixpa.com/blog/sell-stock-photos

https://expertphotography.com/best-stock-photo-sites/

https://hearmefolks.com/how-to-make-money-selling-photos-of-yourself/

Positives: Easy to do.

Negatives: Oversaturated market, not much money to be made.

Cost: 1/5 – Should not cost you anything.

Difficulty Level: 1-5. This is easy to learn.

Profit Potential: $0.02 per image per month with stock photos, while professionals make $0.05–$0.25 per image per month.

Selling video

Just like selling photos, you can sell stock videos to be used by others for commercial purposes.

These sites include but are not limited to the following:

Adobe Stock - https://stock.adobe.com/

Shutterstock - https://www.shutterstock.com/

Pond5 - https://www.pond5.com/

Positives: Easy to do.

Negatives: Oversaturated market, not much money to be made.

Cost: 1/5 – Should not cost you anything.

Difficulty Level: 1–5. This is easy to learn.

Profit Potential: $ 0 to $100 a month. Experts can earn over $1,000 a month.

2. Selling music

You can also sell your stock music online to be used for commercial purposes.

These sites include but are not limited to the following:

AudioJungle – https://audiojungle.net/

Shutterstock – https://www.shutterstock.com/

Pond5 – https://www.pond5.com/

Roqstar – https://www.roqstar.io/

Epidemic Sound – https://www.epidemicsound.com/for-artists/

Positives: Easy to do.

Negatives: Oversaturated market, your music has to stand out.

Cost: 1/5 – Should not cost you anything.

Difficulty Level: 1–5. This is easy to learn.

Profit Potential: $ 0 to over $1,000+ a month.

Chapter 12:

Selling Crafts

Many people enjoy making crafts, and this can be something you can sell online. For this side hustle, you create an e-commerce page on sites like Esty and sell your handy crafts. Or you can sell the item at various craft fairs or to retailers.

Steps to selling crafts on Etsy:

Step 1: Create a seller page on Etsy – https://www.etsy.com/.

Step 2: Post the craft items you want to sell on Etsy. Please note that Etsy charges fees for listings and a percentage of the profits.

Step 3: Market the products through social media using paid ads. Be careful with this, as it can be costly.

Positives: Get paid for something you enjoy doing.

Negatives: Oversaturated market, you have to learn how to market the product.

Cost: 2/5 – Cost of the product and to market the product online or to rent a booth at a craft fair.

Difficulty Level: 2-5. Must learn how to market the product.

Profit Potential: $ 0 to over $1,000+ a month.

Chapter 13:

Sports & Fitness as a Side Hustle

For those who like sports and or fitness, you can do a side hustle under this topic. Below you can learn more about this topic.

Teach a sport

Many people are skilled in a sport, swimming or martial art, and can teach this skill to people looking to learn this skill. An example of this is my father, Murray, who is close to his 80's and has been making a good living teaching others to run for years.

Where to look for clients:

1. Teach out of a community organization like YMCA or a private club 2.   Post on social media

3. Word of Mouth

4. Social media ads

5. Local community ads **Positives:** Get paid for something you enjoy doing.

Negatives: If doing this on your own, you have to learn how to market your service. Dealing with brady kids and bad parents in some cases.

Cost: 1/5 – It should cost you only gas money if you are traveling. If paying for ads, it could be additional cost.

Difficulty Level: 1-5. As you already have the skill.

Profit Potential: $20 an hour to over $200 plus an hour for experts teaching a skill.

Coach on a sports team or individual athletes

Many sports teams need coaches including private clubs who want good experienced coaches for a paid fee.

Where to find work:

1. Look for private clubs looking to hire coaches

2. Look at communities' organization looking to hire coaches

3. Look for people looking to hire coaches for 1on1 sessions **Positives:** Get paid for something you enjoy doing.

Negatives: Dealing with brady kids and bad parents in some cases.

Cost: 1/5 – It should cost you only gas money if you are traveling.

Difficulty Level: 1-5. As you already have the skill.

Profit Potential: $20 an hour to over $200 plus an hour for experts teaching one-on-one.

Referee a sport

Just like coaches, many leagues need referees to referee sporting events.

Where to find work:

1. Look for private clubs looking to hire coaches

2. Look at community organization looking to hire coaches **Positives:** Get paid for something you like.

Negatives: Dealing with brady kids and bad parents in some cases.

Cost: 1/5 – It should cost you only gas money if you are traveling.

Difficulty Level: 1–5. As you already have the skill.

Profit Potential: $20 an hour to over $200 plus an hour for advanced leagues in some locations.

Personal Trainer or teach a Fitness Class

Many people have developed excellent skills in fitness and can profit by teaching and coaching others in this area.

My personal experience

In my early 20s, I did this and made decent money personal training clients at gyms and homes.

Some areas require certifications.

Some areas require the person to be certified and or to have their first aid/CPR.

Where to find work:

1. Train or teach fitness classes out of gyms.

2. Train or teach out of a community organization like YMCA.

3. Train people at their homes by finding clients on your own.

Positives: Get paid for something you like.

Negatives: Dealing with bad clients.

Cost: 1/5 – It should cost you only gas money if you are traveling. If finding clients on your own to market your service, then that cost.

Difficulty Level: 1–5. As you already have the skill.

Profit Potential: $30 an hour to over $100 plus an hour for advanced fitness experts.

Chapter 14:

Hairdresser/Barber & Beauty Care as a Side Hustle

D o you have skills in beauty care? You can make side hustle money with those particular skills.

Types of beauty care side hustles:

1. Hair Stylist
2. Hairdressers
3. Color Specialist
4. Wig or Weave Specialist
5. Barber
6. Manicurists and Pedicurists
7. Make-up Artist

8. Esthetician
9. Electrologist
10. Stylist Note that in some regions, you might need a local or state license to work in the above areas.

Where to find work:

1. In salons or barber shops and other related places.
2. At your home or the client's home **Positives:** Get paid for something you enjoy doing.

Negatives: Dealing with bad clients, some areas of beauty do not pay high.

Cost: 1/5 – It should cost you only gas money if you are traveling. If you are working for yourself, equipment for things like Electrolysis can be expensive. Also, any advertising costs.

Difficulty Level: 1–5. As you already have the skill.

Profit Potential: Hairstylists/Hairdressers - $20 – $300 plus, Color Specialist - $25 an hour on average, Wig or Weave Specialists - $14 - $28 an hour on average, Barbers - $15 - $30, Manicurists and Pedicurists - $17 to $22 an hour on average, Make-up Artist $25 - $28 an hour on average, Esthetician make $25 - $35 an hour on average,

Electrologist $40 - $50 an hour on average. Stylists make $20 - $30 an hour on average.

Chapter 15:

Pet Side Hustles

M any people love animals and pets, and there are many ways to profit from the love of animals.

Dog walker

This is where you walk 1 or many dogs for busy pet owners.

How to find clients:

1. Local ads or flyers door to door.
2. Facebook Market Place ad.
3. Yelp or similar local business pages.
4. Develop email lists.
5. Posting in local Facebook community groups.

6. Local classified Ads/Craigslist.

7. Facebook Business Page Posts.

8. Posting with permission at pet stores, animal clinics, groomers and pet trainers.

Positives: Get paid for something you enjoy doing.

Negatives: Dealing with bad pet owners, low profits.

Cost: 1/5 – It should cost you nothing except if you travel to a client, then gas money. Also, any advertising costs.

Difficulty Level: 1-5. As you already have the skill.

Profit Potential: $15 - $20 an hour.

Pet Sitters

People who go on vacation or people who work long hours need pet sitters either in their client's homes or to pet sit in their own homes. I knew of someone who did this and made just under $40,000 annually out of her home.

How to find clients:

1. Local ads or flyers door to door.

2. Facebook Market Place ad.

3. Yelp or similar local business pages.

4. Develop email lists.

5. Posting in local Facebook community groups.

6. Local classified Ads/Craigslist.

7. Facebook Business Page Posts.

8. Posting with permission at pet stores, animal clinics, groomers, and pet trainers.

Positives: Get paid for something you enjoy doing.

Negatives: Dealing with bad pet owners.

Cost: 2/5 – Cost of pet food and supplies, if you travel to client sites gas money. Also, any advertising costs.

Difficulty Level: 1-5 – Should be easy for animal lovers.

Profit Potential: If per hour $15 on average. If pets stay with you all day, then many charge $20-$30 per day. If you have the capacity to take care of multiple pets safely and can do 5 pets per day, you could make an extra $100 to $150 per day. If you did that all year at $500 - $750 a week, that could be an extra $25,000 to $37,500 per year.

Pet Groomer

Grooming dogs, for many, is hard and time-consuming, and prefer to have a pro pet groomer doing this for them.

This side hustle can be done either on your own or at a groomers.

If you are on your own, then clients can come to you, or you can come to them. Keeping in mind equipment and the messiness of the job.

How to find clients if you work for yourself

1. Local ads or flyers door to door.
2. Facebook Market Place ad.
3. Yelp/Google page.
4. Posting with permission at pet stores, animal clinics, and pet trainers.
5. Develop email lists.
6. Posting in local Facebook community groups.
7. Local classified Ads/Craigslist.
8. Facebook Business Page Posts.

Positives: Get paid for something you enjoy doing.

Negatives: Dealing with bad pet owners or none behaving dogs.

Cost: 2/5 – Cost of cleaning supplies, if you travel to client sites gas money. Also, any advertising costs.

Difficulty Level: 1-5 as long as you have training. If no skills, you will need to learn this properly.

Profit Potential: This profession can vary from $15 an hour to $50+ an hour for experts working for themselves.

Pet Trainer

Some dogs need behavior training and hire a pet trainer to improve their dog's behavior. This side hustle can be done either on your own, at a dog trainer center, or sometimes at a community center. If you are on your own, then clients can come to you, or you can come to them.

How to find clients if you work for yourself

1. Facebook Market Place ad.
2. Local classified ads.
3. Yelp/Google page.
4. Posting with permission at pet stores, animal clinics, and pet groomers.
5. Develop email lists.
6. Posting in local Facebook community groups.
7. Facebook Business Page Posts.

Positives: Get paid for something you enjoy doing.

Negatives: Dealing with bad pet owners or none behaving dogs. Not a lot of money to be made.

Cost: 1/5 – Only gas money if you travel to client site. Also, any advertising costs.

Difficulty Level: 1-5 as long as you have training. If no skills, you will need to learn this properly.

Profit Potential: This profession can vary from $15 an hour to $25+ an hour for experts working for themselves.

Chapter 16:

Photographer and Videographer Side Hustles

Many people have talents in photography and videography and that can be used to make money as a side hustle. On a personal note, my wife worked in Photography and Videography before we got married and still does the occasional videos for clients.

Types of clients looking for Photographers and Videographers

1. Weddings
2. Religious or cultural milestone events
3. New baby photos
4. Family photos

5. Business headshots photos for business professionals
6. YouTube commercial requiring videographer

How to find clients if you work for yourself

1. Facebook Market Place ad.
2. Local classified ads.
3. Yelp/Google pages.
4. For wedding clients referrals from other wedding professionals like wedding planners, caterers, florists.
5. Posting in local Facebook community groups.
6. Facebook Business Page Posts.

Positives: Get paid for something you enjoy doing.

Negatives: Dealing with bad picky clients. On your feet a lot. Lots of competition in some regions.

Cost: 2/5 – Equipment if you do not have as well as maintenance and film for the camera. Any advertising costs.

Difficulty Level: 1-5 as long as you have the skills. If you have no skills, you will need to learn this properly. Also, any advertising costs.

Profit Potential: For photographers, profit can vary from $50 for a headshot to over $10,000 for some weddings, with $5,00 being the average. For Videographers for a simple, quick commercial as low as $500 to over $10,000. For a wedding at the low end, $1,000 to over $5,000 dollars.

Chapter 17:

Food-Related Side Hustles

Many people are passionate about food, and some side hustles under this topic could interest you. Also, many people want healthy home-cooked food and do not have the time to cook and are looking for people to buy food from people who do this.

Catering Meals

As long as your area does not have bylaws against preparing meals for others, you could do catering for clients, from serving 1 meal to larger volumes depending on your skills, and kitchen capacity.

How to find clients if you work for yourself

1. Local classified ads.
2. Yelp/Google pages.
3. Word of Mouth.
4. Develop email lists.
5. Posting in local Facebook community groups.
6. Local classified Ads/Craigslist.
7. Facebook Business Page Posts.

Positives: Get paid for something you enjoy doing.

Negatives: Dealing with bad picky clients.

Cost: 2/5 – Cost of wear and tear on your kitchen and buying ingredients. Also, any advertising costs.

Difficulty Level: 1-5 as long as you have the skills.

Profit Potential: This will vary from a few hundred bucks for serving a small meal to

thousands of dollars for catering to a big event.

High-end Waiter or Bartender

In some regions, some waiters and bartenders on tips can make very good money working in high-end restaurants, hotels, and nightclubs.

Positives: Lots of tips under the table can be made.

Negatives: Dealing with rude customers. On your feet a lot.

Cost: 1/5 – Just gas money to get to work.

Difficulty Level: 2-5 as you have to face consistently demanding clients quickly and efficiently.

Profit Potential: This will vary from $20 an hour in tips to hundreds of dollars an hour in the right location and region of the country.

Chapter 18:

Entertainment Side Hustles

Many people enjoy the world of entertainment, and there are different options for side hustles in this field.

DJ

If you have skills as a DJ, you can find employment in clubs or as a private party DJ. Many private events and businesses need to hire DJs, so that could be an option. Or you could go at one your own.

How to find clients if you work for yourself

1. Facebook Market Place ad.
2. Local classified ads.
3. Yelp/Google pages.

4. Word of Mouth.

5. Advertise with Wedding Photographers, Florists, & Wedding musicians and DJs to mutually promote each other.

6. Posting in local Facebook community groups.

7. Facebook Business Page Posts.

Positives: Doing something you enjoy.

Negatives: Dealing with rude clients. On your feet a lot.

Cost: 3/5 – If you are on your own and have to buy equipment, it could get expensive. Also, any advertising costs.

Difficulty Level: 1-5, as you should have the skills already.

Profit Potential: From the low end of $50 to over $1,000 an event. With the average being about $400 an event. With some top DJs making way over 6 figures an event.

Wedding band

Do you play an instrument, or can sing? Then joining a wedding band with this talent could be a great way to earn extra cash.

Positives: Doing something you enjoy.

Negatives: On your feet a lot.

Cost: 1/5 – As you most likely have the instrument, then just gas money.

Difficulty Level: 1-5, as you should have the skills already.

Profit Potential: From a low end of $100 a night to over $1,000 a night, with top performers making much more.

Children's birthday party performer

Some parents hire children's performers to perform at their kid's birthday parties. This can include clowns, magicians, people dressed in costumes or making a themed birthday party like a Disney princess party.

How to find clients if you work for yourself

1. Facebook Market Place ad.
2. Advertising in parents' centric media.
3. Asking children's clothing stores, toy stores, and other kid-centric retailers to put up a paid advertisement.
4. Local classified ads.
5. Create a YouTube page to advertise your services.
6. Yelp/Google pages.
7. Word of Mouth.

8. Posting in local Facebook community groups.
9. Facebook Business Page Posts.

Positives: Making kids happy.

Negatives: dealing with bratty kids, mean parents, on your feet a lot.

Cost: 2/5 – Cost of costumes/themes and Party Supplies. Cost of marketing if need be.

Difficulty Level: 1-5 - Easy to learn how to entertain kids.

Profit Potential: $100 to over $1000 for performance plus tips.

Wedding planner

Are you great at organizing people and events? Then a wedding planner might be right for you.

How to find clients if you work for yourself

1. Facebook Market Place ad.
2. Local classified ads.
3. Yelp/Google pages.
4. Word of Mouth.

5. Advertise with Wedding Photographers, Florists, & Wedding musicians and DJs to mutually promote each other.

6. Posting in local Facebook community groups.

7. Facebook Business Page Posts.

Positives: Doing something you enjoy.

Negatives: Dealing with rude clients. On your feet a lot.

Cost: 1/5 – Gas money to get to locations. Cost of marketing if need be.

Difficulty Level: 3-5 - as many take out their frustration on wedding planners.

Profit Potential: From the low end of a few hundred dollars to over $10,000 for a wedding.

Chapter 19:

Clothes Alteration as a Side Hustle

Most people today cannot hem, fix, or alter clothes and need someone to do this for them. You could open your own home alteration business to help clients needing this service.

How to find clients if you work for yourself

1. Put a sign out on your lawn or property.
2. Facebook Market Place ad.
3. Local classified ads.
4. Yelp/Google pages.
5. Word of Mouth.
6. Network with clothing stores and bridal boutiques.

7. Develop email lists.

8. Posting in local Facebook community groups.

9. Local classified Ads/Craigslist.

10. Facebook Business Page Posts.

Positives: Doing something you have a skill in.

Negatives: Dealing with rude clients and the privacy of people entering your home.

Cost: 1/5 – If you do not have sowing equipment, then this could go up to a 2. Cost of marketing if need be.

Difficulty Level: 1-5 – As long as you have the skill needed.

Profit Potential: From the low end of $15 to over $500 an item for complex seaming.

Chapter 20:

Handyman Services

M ost people cannot fix or build things themselves and rely on a handyman to fix or build things for them.

General handyman

General handymen do many different handy jobs for people, from building, fixing things and light plumbing and electrical. They do anything, not including things that require a license, such as an electrician or plumber.

How to find clients if you work for yourself

1. Word of Mouth.
2. Facebook Market Place ad.
3. Local classified ads.
4. Yelp/Google pages.

Positives: Doing something you already are skilled in.

Negatives: Dealing with rude clients and the privacy of entering people's homes. Also, very physically tasking.

Cost: 2/5 – Tools and upkeep of tools. Cost of marketing if need be.

Difficulty Level: 2-5 – Even if you have the skill, it is a physically demanding job.

Profit Potential: At the low end of $20 to over $100 an hour in some regions.

Ikea furniture

Many people buy build-it-yourself furniture and cannot build it themselves, so they hire people who can do this for them. If you are good at building furniture why not make money doing this?

How to find clients if you work for yourself

1. Referral by furniture stores – Network with stores and tell them you will pay a referral fee to the store.
2. Word of Mouth.
3. Facebook Market Place ad.
4. Local classified ads.
5. Yelp/Google pages.

Positives: Doing something you already are skilled in.

Negatives: Dealing with rude clients and the privacy of entering people's homes.

Cost: 1/5 – Should be 1 as long as you have the right tools. Cost of marketing if need be.

Difficulty Level: 1-5 – As long as you have the existing skills.

Profit Potential: $40 to over $200 for each piece depending on where you live and how complex the furniture is.

Chapter 21:

Cleaning Services

Many people, either through no time or not liking germs, need to hire cleaning services for many different types of jobs. Below you will learn about a bunch of side hustles you can do if you have cleaning skills.

Different cleaning services

Residential

Many people, at some point, have hired a cleaner for their homes.

Commercial Cleaning Service

This is where cleaners are contracted to clean a business, usually after hours.

House Staging Cleaners

This is where you clean a house preparing to be sold on the real estate market.

House Moving Cleaners

This is when you clean a house when people are moving out before the new owner/renter moves in.

How to find clients if you work for yourself

1. For house staging and house moving network with real estate agents or property management companies.

2. For commercial cleaners' network with businesses advertising your services.

3. Word of Mouth.

4. Facebook Market Place ad.

5. Local classified ads.

6. Yelp/Google pages.

Positives: Easy to start and needed in many places.

Negatives: Dealing with rude clients and the privacy of entering people's homes and businesses. Dealing with other people's germs, sometimes false accusations of theft.

Cost: 2/5 – cleaning supplies, especially for commercial and staging homes. Cost of marketing if need be.

Difficulty Level: 3-5 – Takes a lot of hard work.

Profit Potential:

Residential – $10 to $30 an hour, depending on location.

Commercial Cleaning Service – $25 to over $100 an hour, depending on location.

House Staging Cleaners – $200 a house on the low end to over $1,000 a house in some areas and for big homes.

House Moving Cleaners – $200 a house on the low end to over $1,000 a house in some areas and for big homes.

Pet Waste Removal

Many people do not want to get rid of their pet's waste on their property or, unfortunately even other people's pets' waste, so they hire someone to do this for them.

How to find clients if you work for yourself

1. Network with Pet stores, animal clinics, pet groomers, pet trainers about putting out your flyer. Offer them a referral bonus.
2. Facebook Market Place ad.
3. Local classified ads.
4. Yelp/Google pages.
5. Word of Mouth.

Positives: Easy to start and needed in many places.

Negatives: Dealing with rude clients and the privacy of entering people's yards. Dealing with the possibility of animals. Very dirty messy job.

Cost: 2/5 – Industrial cleaning supplies. Cost of marketing if need be.

Difficulty Level: 2-5 – easy work but not for the faint of heart when it comes to germs.

Profit Potential: $10 to over $50 a session, with some clients paying a weekly or monthly fee.

Junk Removal

People and businesses in the process of moving or wanting to do a major clean up sometimes need a junk removal company to remove large amounts of stuff quickly.

How to find clients if you work for yourself

1. Social media posts.
2. Facebook Market Place ad.
3. Local classified ads.
4. Yelp/Google pages.
5. Word of Mouth.
6. Network with real estate agents, real estate stagers.

Positives: Easy business to learn.

Negatives: Cost of truck, dealing with bad clients, over-saturated market in some locations.

Cost: 4/5 – If you do not have a truck, the cost of a truck, the cost of gas money, cost to advertise if need be.

Difficulty Level: 3-5 – Very hard physical work.

Profit Potential: $600 per truck load on average depending on location and how much junk you are howling.

Chapter 22:

Home Organizing Services

A re you good at organizing your home? Then a home organizing side hustle might be right for you.

How to find clients if you work for yourself

1. Social media posts.
2. Facebook Market Place ad.
3. Local classified ads.
4. Yelp/Google pages.
5. Word of Mouth.
6. Network with real estate agents, real estate stagers.

Positives: No start-up costs other than advertising.

Negatives: Dealing with bad clients, over-saturated market in some locations.

Cost: 1/5 – the cost of gas money, cost to advertise if need be.

Difficulty Level: 1-5 – If you already have outstanding organization home skills.

Profit Potential: $30 to over $100 an hour depending on the location and size of the job.

Chapter 23:

Yard and Outdoor Cleaning Services

There are many kinds of yard and outdoor cleaning side hustles, and below, you will learn about many of them.

Gutter Cleaning

An interesting cleaning side hustle that many do not think about is gutter cleaning. This is where you clean a person's house gutters to prevent them from getting clogged so that when it rains, it can properly drain water and prevent water damage.

How to find clients if you work for yourself

1. Door-to-door asking people if they need this.
2. Local flyers.
3. Facebook Market Place ad.
4. Local classified ads.
5. Yelp/Google pages.
6. Word of Mouth.

Positives: In some areas, a big need.

Negatives: Dealing with rude clients and the privacy of entering people's yards. Very dirty, messy job.

Cost: 2/5 – Buying equipment needed for this could cost over $1,000, including buying a Ladder, Wet/dry vacuum, Outdoor gloves, Pressure washer, Leaf blower, Grabbers or Scoopers, Collection containers, and Liquid cleaners. Also, you might need to buy a truck or big car if you do not have one to transport your equipment. If you advertise, there would be the cost of advertising as well.

Difficulty Level: 3-5 – hard labor and a very messy job.

Profit Potential: $75 to over $500 a house, depending on the location and size of the house.

Power Washing

Many people, over time, get a dirty patio, balcony, driveway, and another similar outdoor area that needs cleaning and hire a professional to help them.

How to find clients if you work for yourself

1. Door-to-door asking people if they need this.
2. Local flyers.
3. Facebook Market Place ad.
4. Local classified ads.
5. Yelp/Google pages.
6. Word of Mouth.

Positives: In some areas, a big need.

Negatives: Dealing with rude clients and the privacy of entering people's yards. Very dirty, messy job.

Cost: 3/5 – Buying equipment could be $1,000 to over $5,000, not including buying a truck if you do not have one. Cost of buying a pressure washer, high-pressure water hoses, and nozzles for your washer. You will also need to buy chemicals and cleaners. Also, a truck if you do not have one. If you advertise, there would be the cost of advertising as well.

Difficulty Level: 3-5 – hard labor and a very messy job.

Profit Potential: $200 to over $500 a job, depending on the location, size of the job, and difficulty of the job.

Pool Cleaning Service

Most people do not clean their pools and require a pool cleaning service.

How to find clients if you work for yourself

1. Facebook Market Place ad.
2. Local classified ads.
3. Yelp/Google pages.
4. Word of Mouth.

Positives: Decent money to be made.

Negatives: Dealing with bad clients, making a mistake that damages a pool, being locked out of a pool fence.

Cost: 3/5 – Chemicals can get costly, cost of gas money, cost to advertise if need be.

Difficulty Level: 2-5 – Learning to clean properly if you do not know how to. Out in the sun or cold, handily chemicals.

Profit Potential: $100 to over $250 a month clients pay to have their pool cleaned every week.

Mowing Lawns

This old-school side hustle many people think of teenagers but can be a great way to make quick cash in the evenings.

How to find clients if you work for yourself

1. Door-to-door asking people if they need this.
2. Local flyers.
3. Facebook Market Place ad.
4. Local classified ads.
5. Yelp/Google pages.
6. Word of Mouth.

Positives: Easy to start and do.

Negatives: Dealing with rude clients and the privacy of entering people's yards. Hard work. In some areas, a very oversaturated market. Cold in some regions or hot in some regions.

Cost: 2/5 – Lawnmower if you do not have one or wear and tear on your equipment and fuel. Cost of marketing if need be.

Difficulty Level: 2-5 – Hard work, time-consuming, and better-paying side gigs.

Profit Potential: Average $40 to $50 a visit.

Chapter 24:

Physical Jobs as a Side Hustle

A re you strong and in good shape? Then there are side hustles that can make use of your strength.

Moving Service

Many people do not have the strength or time to move or move furniture, so they hire someone to do this for them. For this side hustle, you can work for someone with a costly truck or do it on your own.

How to find clients if you work for yourself

1. Posting in local Facebook community groups.

2. Network with Real Estate brokers, mortgage specialists.
3. Facebook Market Place ads.
4. Local classified ads.
5. Yelp/Google pages.
6. Word of Mouth.

Positives: Potential to do well if you have your own business and can outsource the heavy work.

Negatives: Dealing with rude clients.

Cost: 5/5 – If there is no truck, then this will be very expensive to get one. Also, wear and tear on vehicles. Insurance as breakables is very common. In addition, the cost of hiring a crew for big jobs. Cost of marketing if need be.

Difficulty Level: 5-5 – a very physical back-breaking job.

Profit Potential: $100 for moving furniture to over $3000 plus tips in some regions for a whole family move.

Chapter 25:

Teaching and Tutoring Side Hustles

There are different ways to earn money teaching and tutoring as a side hustle, and below, you will learn about some of the most common.

Tudor

Many parents in school want to give their kids an edge by hiring a tutor to improve their grades.

If you are good at specific subjects, especially math and science, and can teach this to others, then working as a tutor could be a great side hustle for you. You can either work for a tutoring firm, or you can work for yourself for more profit.

How to find clients if you work for yourself

1. Posting in local Facebook parent community groups.
2. Network with stores that sell kids products and offer a referral fee.
3. Facebook Market Place ads.
4. Local classified ads.
5. Yelp/Google pages.
6. Word of Mouth.

Positives: Demand in some locations.

Negatives: Dealing with overbearing parents and misbehaved kids. Might require preparation.

Cost: 1/5 – Should be just gas money if you travel to the kid's site. Also, any advertising costs if need be.

Difficulty Level: 2-5 – If you have the skills, then just the aggravation of kids and parents. Cost of marketing if need be.

Profit Potential: $20 to over $60 an hour.

Music Teacher

Many parents want to teach their kids how to play music, especially things like piano, guitar and singing. If you are a trained musician, you can make money with this side hustle by either having a home studio or going to clients' homes.

How to find clients if you work for yourself

1. Network with music stores and offer a referral fee.
2. Posting in local Facebook parent community groups.
3. Network with stores that sell kids' products and offer a referral fee.
4. Facebook Market Place ads.
5. Local classified ads.
6. Yelp/Google pages.
7. Word of Mouth.

Positives: Do something you enjoy doing.

Negatives: Dealing with overbearing parents and misbehaved kids. Might require preparation.

Cost: 1/5 – Instrument maintenance or gas money if you travel to the kid's site. Cost of marketing if need be.

Difficulty Level: 2-5 – If you have the skills, then just the aggravation of kids and parents.

Profit Potential: $25 to over $60 an hour.

Teaching English

English is a language used around the world, and many countries are looking for virtual English teachers. Some teaching firms require experience and education and others do not. The salaries are low, but there are many companies you can teach with and below you will find different ones.

Also, there are many companies out there, so do your research.

1. Cambly – https://www.cambly.com/en/tutors?lang=en

2. PalFish – https://www.ipalfish.com/klian/web/dist/palfish/teacher.html

3. Magic Ears – https://t.mmears.com/v2/

4. Vip Kid – https://www.vipkid.com/teach

5. Qkids – https://teacher.qkids.com/job **Positives:** Many jobs to be found.

Negatives: Pre and Post class preparation, low pay.

Cost: 1/5 – No cost needed.

Difficulty Level: 2-5 – Teaching is not easy but at least you can teach from the comfort of your home.

Profit Potential: $10 – $28 an hour.

Community College Instructor

Many community colleges need online or in-person instructors for a variety of subjects.

Some of these classes are just looking for industry experts in a particular topic. For example, if you are a personal trainer, a college might hire you to teach a class about fitness.

Where to find community college instructor jobs?

The best place to look at is a community college website and see what kind of instructors they are looking to hire. Another place is to look on Indeed.com or https://www.higheredjobs.com/ and look to see if there are any classes you would be qualified to teach.

Positives: Make extra money off something you are an expert in.

Negatives: Pre and Post class preparation.

Cost: 1/5 – No cost needed.

Difficulty Level: 2-5 – Teaching is not easy.

Profit Potential: $40-$50 an hour on average.

Chapter 26:

Affiliate Marketing as a Side Hustle

D o you have a website or blog with decent web traffic? Then affiliate marketing might be a decent side hustle for you. Affiliate marketing is where you advertise a product or service on your website or blog, and if someone purchases the product or service, you get paid a percentage of the sales.

How to find an Affiliate product and services to market

1. Check a company's website

Many firms list that they are looking for affiliates to market their products or services. The great thing about this is that you pay no fees as you work directly with the company looking for affiliates. Follow the instructions they list on their sites on how to become an affiliate.

2. Use a main Affiliate Networks Site

These are sites that act as middlemen connecting you to affiliate businesses. They take a cut, and there could be upfront fees of over $3,000, but it could be worth it to save you time and find you a high-paying client. Below are some firms to look at.

AvantLink - https://www.avantlink.com/

AWIN - https://www.awin.com/us

CJ - https://www.cj.com/

Rakuten Advertising - https://rakutenadvertising.com/affiliate/

ShareASale - https://www.shareasale.com/info/

Positives: Make extra money off something you already have, which is a website with traffic.

Negatives: Cost if you use a main affiliate network. Some people may need to be more comfortable commercializing their website or blogs.

Cost: 4/5 – This can be a 1 if you find your own affiliate, but if you use a Main Affiliate Networks Site, this would be a 4 out of 5.

Difficulty Level: 2-5 – Might be hard to set up if someone is not tech savvy.

Profit Potential: $10 a month to over $100,000 a month.

Chapter 27:

Diving and Delivering as a Side Hustle

One of the most common side hustles is being a driver or delivery person. These roles do not pay well but they are easily available in most locations.

Uber or Lyft driver

This might be the most common side hustle people think of today and the reason is it is easy to do and start as long as you have a car.

Major Driving Sites

Uber – **https://www.uber.com/**

Lyft – https://www.lyft.com/drive-with-lyft

Positives: Easy to do and start and flexible. Lots of work in most areas.

Negatives: Low pay, wear and tear on your car, dealing with bad or dangerous passengers.

Cost: 2/5 – Cost of fuel and wear and tear on your car.

Difficulty Level: 1–5 – Very easy to do.

Profit Potential: Depending on location the average uber driver makes $15 an hour compared to the average Lyft driver making $18 an hour.

Delivery Driver

Many people and businesses rely on delivery people to deliver items to them safely, and this has expanded the need for drivers. The jobs do not pay well but are easy to do and start, and most of all there are tons of them available.

Where to find delivery gigs

1. UPS – https://www.jobs-ups.com/package-delivery-driver

2. FedEx - https://careers.fedex.com/express-delivery-driver

3. Amazon Flex - https://flex.amazon.com/

4. Restaurants - Many restaurants hire delivery people.

5. Retailers - Some retailers like furniture and electronics hire delivery people.

6. DoorDash - https://dasher.doordash.com/en-us

7. Instacart - https://shoppers.instacart.com/

8. SHIPT - https://www.shipt.com/be-a-driver

9. Postmates - https://deliver.postmates.com/

10. GrubHub - https://driver.grubhub.com/

Positives: Easy to do and start and flexible. Lots of work in most areas.

Negatives: Low pay, dealing with rude people, for many roles you have to supply the vehicle.

Cost: 2/5 - Cost of fuel and wear and tear on your car if you are in a role that requires you to supply your vehicle.

Difficulty Level: 1-5 - Very easy to do.

Profit Potential: Depending on the location the average delivery driver makes $19 per hour plus tips.

Chapter 28:

Easy Miscellaneous Small Paying Side Hustles

M any other types of side hustles do not fall under any specific categories so that I will list them under this chapter. These are easy to do gigs but are small paying side hustles.

Mystery Shopper

A Mystery Shopper is hired to evaluate customer experience given by a company usually by going in person to a business usually a retailer, hotels, restaurants or by calling into a contact center plus many other businesses that want to determine their service levels.

Where to find Myster Shopper gigs

1. A Closer Look - https://a-closer-look.com/mystery-shopper-headquarters

2. BestMark - https://www.bestmark.com/become-a-mystery-shopper/

3. Market Force - https://www.marketforce.com/become-a-shopper

4. Perception Strategies - https://www.perstrat.com/shopper-app

5. Second to none - https://www.second-to-none.com/become-a-mystery-shopper/

Positives: Make extra money with no skills needed.

Negatives: Low paying gigs.

Cost: 1/5 – Only travel cost.

Difficulty Level: 1–5 – Super easy to do.

Profit Potential: $5 - $20 per mystery shopping gig on average depending on location and what you are reviewing.

Paid Market Research Studies

Market research firms will pay a person for their opinions on a variety of topics from food, media, to even politics. Some firm requires you pay a fee to join and I would ignore any firm where you have to pay to sign-up. Also, some firms pay in gift certificates rather than cash.

Where to find paid market research gigs

1. American Consumer Opinion - https://www.acop.com

2. Ipsos i-Say - https://www.ipsosisay.com/en-us

3. Nielsen - https://panels.nielsen.com/panels-and-surveys/

4. Swagbucks - https://www.swagbucks.com/discover/sign-ups

5. Toluna - https://www.toluna.com/register

Positives: Make extra money with no skills needed.

Negatives: Low paying gigs.

Cost: 1/5 – Only travel cost.

Difficulty Level: 1-5 – Super easy to do.

Profit Potential: $1 to over $50 in cash or gift card per survey depending on location and what you are doing market research for and what survey company you are working for.

Taking Part in a Clinical Trial

Many pharmaceutical or medical research companies will pay you to take part in a clinical trial.

When looking for a trail, make sure you are comfortable with the safety and the reputation of the organization conduction the trial and make sure it is a paid study.

Where to find paid clinical trial gigs

1. Check at medical research and pharmaceutical sites for paid studies.

2. My Local Study - This site lists trials - https://mylocalstudy.com/

3. National Institutes of Health - On the site you can find paid trial - https://www.nih.gov/health-information/nih-clinical-research-trials-you/finding-clinical-trial

4. Paid Clinical Trials Near Me - This site lists trials - https://paidclinicaltrialsnearme.com/

5. Parexel - https://www.parexel.com/participate

Positives: Make extra money with no skills needed, helping in medical and drug research.

Negatives: Be careful about safety! Some trials are low-paying gigs.

Cost: 1/5 – Only travel cost

Difficulty Level: 2-5 – Some trials can be a bit dangerous.

Profit Potential: $50 to $300 a day for participating in a trial.

Selling Blood

In some countries you can sell your blood as there is a huge need for blood in many locations.

Where to find places to sell blood?

1. BioLife - https://info.biolifeplasma.com/new-plasma-donation-0722

2. BSC - https://www.biospecialty.com/

3. Octa Pharma Plasma - https://www.octapharmaplasma.com/

Positives: Make extra money with no skills needed, helping people who need blood.

Negatives: Be careful about safety! Low payment.

Cost: 1/5 – Only travel cost.

Difficulty Level: 2-5 – If you are not healthy do not do this!

Profit Potential: On average $50 to $75 per blood donation session.

Be an extra in a movie or a TV show

In some geographical areas they need extras for both TV and movies. Basically, you are used as a background person.

How to find extra gigs

Look for a reputable casting agency in your local area. You can search on Google and look for reviews and better business bureau reports to ensure the honesty of the agency. In your application a headshot most likely will be needed. Also make sure you do not pay anything!

Positives: Make extra money with no skills needed.

Negatives: Long days, on your feet all day or waiting around doing nothing until your scene.

Cost: 1/5 – Only travel cost.

Difficulty Level: 1-5 – Super easy gig.

Profit Potential: $100 to $200 a day.

Chapter 29:

Side Hustles Marketing Tips

In previous chapters, I wrote about different ways to market some of the side hustles. To expand upon this, I will explain more about how to do some of the major marketing techniques that apply to many of the side hustles that require customer acquisition.

Facebook Business Page Posts

For many of the service-related side hustles, I recommend creating a Facebook business page and adding as many local people as you can to the page. Creating a page is free and easy, just make sure it looks professional. From this page post things about your services. Be original and add personal things about the service as well as posting lots of videos and pictures.

Posting in local Facebook community groups

Many local community groups on Facebook allow businesses to post about their services. Do your research as local groups could be a great free way to post about your services.

Local classified ads/Craigslist

Old school classified ads or online classifieds like Craigslist might not be for all services but for some if you use it, you could find it as an avenue to find new clients. Keep in mind there is an ad cost, so monitor the cost in terms of what it brings back in profit.

Network with local businesses for referrals

I wrote about this a few times in this book, and there is a reason as some side hustle services could benefit by creating a reference network with other businesses. How this works is you think of a related business and offer either a mutual referral of each other's services or offer the other business cash for any referrals given. An example of this might be if you are a videographer for weddings, and you offer to mutually refer wedding clients to wedding photographers, caters, florists, planners and anything other wedding-related providers. If you find mutual referrals is not working, try the cash alterative of offering

10% of the sale you make from the referral. Many people are money motivated, so this could provide many extra sales for you. Also, you must pay for the referral not only for the moral obligation but also to keep the referrals coming in. To find related services go onto Google and look up local businesses and both call and email them about either mutual referrals or paid referrals.

Google Pages

Google offers free pages for businesses to create, which hits Google's search engine for people looking for local businesses. To create a page simply go to https://www.google.com/business/

and follow the instructions in creating a page including verifying your address with a mail in code to ensure you are local to your business.

Yelp or similar local Business Pages

Yelp or pages like Yelp can create pages to be found by local people looking for services like yours. Some of these sites offer a paid service to be listed higher on their lists. If you have the budget you might try to experiment to see if these pages bring you more clients.

Develop email lists

I highly recommend keeping the contact information of your clients and getting their permission to send them in future email newsletters about your services, including sales, new products or other promotions. As hopefully you did a good job with the customer/client and when they see future things about your business they will buy from you again.

Do an amazing job to build referrals

The most important thing you can do in building up your side hustle business is to do an outstanding job. This will result in the customer/client referring other people to you and get repeat business. Over the years many of my businesses have lived off of referrals from just being consistent, working hard on customer experience and delivering on customer expectations.

Chapter 30:

Expanding Your Side Hustle Business

There comes an exciting time in your tenure in side hustling when you grow to a point where you cannot handle the business coming your way, and you must choose to stick to being a one person operation or become a business that employs your own staff. If you decide to expand your business, you will have to make some key decisions that will allow you to grow effectively.

This chapter will explain how to expand your business the right way.

Create a plan of expansion

You cannot just one day wake up and start expanding your business. It has to be planned out in terms of many key factors that, if implemented the right way, could be the main difference between you being a one-person show making a decent living to a successful business owner making 7-figures a year. The topics below are things you must consider if you want to do a great job expanding your business.

Do the math properly

When expanding, your operating costs will increase, so you have to understand the cost of expanding operation compared to the profits you anticipate you will make with the expansion.

What was once an operation with no overhead might not require you to pay for employee salaries, bookkeeping, marketing, and technology budgets. To ensure your expansion is not a disaster and over your head financially, you might want to start expanding small with one employee and then expanding when you are comfortable with the financials of expansion.

Create a proper website

If you have not created a website, this is something that you will need to do to grow your business. Make sure when creating a website, you get it created with a modern design, and with the use of an SEO-friendly CMS.

Hire sales staff

The most effective way to expand market share for your business will be to hire sales staff to develop new business for your company. This is simple math; if you are able to hire great sales staff who can bring in one million in revenue to your company and repeat this ten times, you will have a team that can bring in over ten million dollars a year in revenue to your company.

Expand marketing efforts

When looking at acquiring more clients, you will need to eventually implement a more sophisticated marketing plan. This will require either hiring a marketing professional or outsourcing this function to professionals. These marketing professionals will be able to expand your client acquisition using advanced SEO, social media, branding, and affiliate marketing to create a funnel of potential leads to you and your team.

Bookkeeping

When you were a small one-person freelancer, your taxes and accounting were kept quite simple. As you expand and grow, the tax and accounting rules and regulations become more complicated, and you will need to hire competent professionals to help guide you to ensure you are paying the correct taxes and ensuring you can get as many tax write-offs as possible.

Continue to focus on the customer experience

Just as it is important as a one-person operation to provide your clients with excellent customer service, you must ensure as you expand that you do not neglect your existing clients and ensure you continue to provide exceptional service to them. In addition, as you expand, all new clients also must continue to be provided with exceptional service. The one thing in my own businesses that has helped fuel expansion and repeat business has been providing exceptional customer service to my clients.

Get the right technology in place

As you expand, you most likely will need the correct technology in place to ensure your expansion that includes the following.

CRM system – A CRM will be important to store all your valuable client data, as well as sending out emails, tracking sales progress, and even project progress. My advice is to shop around to find one that meets your specific needs. I personally like Monday.com, but that is a personal choice, not an endorsement.

IT security – As you expand, keep all your valuable data safe; you must have proper IT security in place to safeguard your business from online scammers and threats.

Outsourcing, if need be

You do not necessarily need to hire staff as you can always outsource in the areas you need help in. Just like you freelance in an area, you too can hire freelancers to work with you on projects or in areas you are not an expert in, like marketing, IT, HR etc.

Retention

As you expand, maintaining and keeping your top talent is a must for any successful enterprise.

The following section will give you the retention strategies to keep your staff happy and to ensure you retain your talent.

Collecting payment

Even when you are a one-person operation, ensuring your client's pay can be an issue in some cases. It is bound to come up where a client delays payment and in some terrible cases does not pay at all. As you expand, collecting from clients will most likely require using professional accounts receivable professionals and in extreme cases collection agencies.

Learn to give up control

As you expand your business you will have to learn how to give up control and multi-task to ensure you have time to focus on expansion. For me, this was very hard to do but necessary if you want to grow and be successful. It will help to hire trustworthy staff who you can reply on.

Chapter 30:

My Own Experiences
& Case Studies

I would be a hypocrite if I did not apply many of the things in my own book on doing side hustles and not have had success. This chapter will detail how I have done well with side hustles, what I did and how I have helped clients also do well with side hustling.

Rinse & Repeat

My technique when it comes to side hustle is to take something I know or can know quickly and then expand that skill and sell it as many times as I can. For example, within one discipline, there can be multiple related disciplines, and each of these disciplines can then be sold as a consulting service. For example, I started in IT recruitment consulting and have expanded in many other job-related services such as healthcare, retail, banking recruitment, and resume, and career coaching, to name a few. From there I will write books on the topic and also teach courses and offer certifications on the same subject. For yourself, make a list of possible ideas, and you will be surprised how many you will think of. Then for each one, slowly add it in as a service your consulting firm can provide.

Side hustles I have personally done

Below is a chart of side hustles I have personally done.

The Side Hustle	Profit I made from different Side Hustles
Freelancing/Consulting	Multiple services including recruitment, resume writing, career services, interview training, content writing, and others all making very good profit over the years.

Writing and publishing books on Amazon	Many years of making very good royalties
Dumpster Diving	When I did it, I averaged $1,000 a month
Renting out a room in my house	When I did this, I made $500 a month
Buying and selling collectables	At my peak I was making $3,000 a month doing this part-time.
Selling and creating courses	Have made decent profit with this
Speaking Engagements	Have made decent profit with this
Doing Market Research Surveys	Have made between $25 - $100+ a survey doing these over the years.
Personal Training Services	When I was younger, I did this, and I was making $3,000 a month and that was many years ago.

Case Studies of Clients I have helped with Side Hustles

Case Study 1

Keith, a firefighter, was not making enough money in his day job and wanted me to create a side hustle strategy to help his family. When speaking with Keith I learned he had worked in the summers cleaning pools when he was in high school and had an extra attic in his house he was not using. My advice was for him to start a pool cleaning service part-time and rent out a room in his attic. After 1 year Keith was making over 6 figures with his pool cleaning business and was making $1,000 a month for renting out his attic to a young couple.

Case Study 2

My client Deborah was middle aged, had limited education and worked full-time during the week in a school cafeteria. Deborah was concerned in retirement she would not be able to afford the cost of living as she was already just barely surviving. When speaking with Deborah, she had a passion for bargain hunting at garage sales and from discount stores and had quite a knowledge of different nick-nacks. I suggested she use this passion and knowledge to buy and sell things from flea markets and resell them on Amazon, Etsy, and eBay. I told her to start small and then expand. I also recommended she try looking at what her neighbors were throwing away and resell items of value. I also told her once she had some profit, she should try Amazon Retail Arbitrage. In a year of working hard part-time Deborah was making $5,000 a month buying things of value at garage sales/flea markets and thrift shops and reselling them on Amazon, Etsy, and eBay. Also, I was delighted to learn she took my passion of doing dumpster diving and was making $1,000 a month finding things for free in the garbage and reselling the items. She also had started doing Amazon Retail Arbitrage and was making $2,500 a month with that technique.

This client I was the happiest for as she was living paycheck to pay-check with fears of retirement and was now making an extra 6 figures a year doing something she had a passion for!

Case Study 3

My 3rd case study is of a software engineer Raj who was living in a high cost of living city and despite making great money as a developer was struggling. This young man had lots of knowledge and passion in his software engineering area of expertise. Seeing his high level of knowledge I suggested that he create both courses and books in his area of expertise. As well as I suggested he create on the side a high-end freelance business in his area of expertise. Within 1 year this client was doing amazing for himself creating a series of online courses on Udemy and related sites and was doing decent sales on Amazon with his book. For this part of his side hustle Raj was making $5,000 a month even past my expectations for him. In addition, his freelance business was pulling in an incredible $10,000 a month. Even more amazing within 3 years Raj had quit his full-time job and had expanded his freelance and courses business and was making $50,000 a month. Raj was the exception to the rule with his killer work epic and knowledge base but amazing what a person can accomplish.

Conclusion

Many people are struggling to make ends meet. Just think about a few generations back when a working class family where the father worked the mom stayed at home and the family still had a house, paid their bills without credit cards and had yearly vacations. Sadly, with inflation and other economic factors many people need extra money to survive. My goal is by reading my book, you have learned some great ways to make money for yourself and or your family.

Everything you need to start side hustling is written in this book. Just follow-it along with hard work, patience, and a positive attitude, you will successfully build your own side hustles.

Best of luck in your side hustles pursuit.

Warm regards, Steven Mostyn If you enjoyed this book, please kindly give it a review on Amazon.

Related Books by Steven Mostyn

1. Recruiting 101: The Fundamentals of Being a Great Recruiter

https://www.amazon.com/Recruiting-101-Fundamentals-Being-Recruiter/dp/0991490029/

2. Job Search: Fundamentals of Effective Job Hunting, Resumes, and Interviews

https://www.amazon.com/Job-Search-Fundamentals-Effective-Interviews/dp/0991490037/https://www.amazon.com/gp/product/0991490037/

3. Resume 101: How to Write an Effective Resume, LinkedIn Profile, and Cover Letter

https://www.amazon.com/Resume-101-Effective-LinkedIn-Profile/dp/0991490002/

4. *Interview Questions and Answers: How to Answer the Most Common Interview Questions*

https://www.amazon.com/Interview-Questions-Answers-Answer-Common/dp/0991490045/

5. *LinkedIn 101*

https://www.amazon.com/LinkedIn-101-Effective-Profile-Business-ebook/dp/B0BWW8W26X/

6. *Freelance 101*

https://www.amazon.com/Freelance-101-Step-Step-Freelancer/dp/B0CFCYWYPN/

WOULD YOU LIKE AN EDGE IN YOUR JOB SEARCH?

My company, Elite Pro Resume Service, can help you land your next Freelance position.

As you know from reading this book, I strongly believe in helping people prepare for a successful freelance job search. I devote the same level of excellence to my clients, providing each one with industry-leading support, personal service, a flawless and professionally edited resume, and a 100% satisfaction guarantee.

The following services are available to job seekers:

- A one-on-one intake session geared toward customizing your resume (No template resumes here!)

- Resume keyword optimization, which increases your chances of standing out on hiring managers' search lists

- Assistance creating impactful LinkedIn profiles, cover letters, executive profiles, and thank you letters

- Interview training and preparation

- Job search training For more information, visit https://www.eliteproresume.com/

or contact me directly at steven@eliteproresume.com.